Critiquing the Modern in Architecture

Written over four decades, *Critiquing the Modern in Architecture* is a collection of essays exploring the ideological and metaphysical core of modern architecture. Author Jaimini Mehta moves architectural modernism from its primarily Eurocentric definition, interrogating the subject from the perspective of a non-Western thought-world. Mehta groups his essays under three key themes: "Rethinking Modernity" explores the ideological underpinnings of the modernity/ modernism binary; "The Idea of Architecture" looks at a number of issues that constitute the timeless and the invariable aspects of architecture against which the prevalent modernist discourse can be critically evaluated; and "On Praxis" looks at three contemporary architects' work and the Vienna Secessionist movement between 1890 and 1918 to articulate a critique of the underpinnings of the modern movement. Providing a new view of the modern in architecture, this book is critical reading for architectural theorists and scholars of modernism.

Jaimini Mehta is a practicing architect and the Honorary Director of the Center for the Study of Urbanism and Architecture in Vadodara, India. His previous books include *Louis I. Kahn, Architect* (1975, co-authored with Romaldo Giurgola), *Rethinking Modernity: Towards Post Rational Architecture* (2011) and *Embodied Vision: Interpreting the Architecture of Fatehpur Sikri* (2014).

"Jaimini Mehta's collection of essays is a must read for those who believe architecture as both a material and intellectual construct is a metropolis of ideas – diverse, complex, challenging, rewarding, and important. Each thought-provoking essay is a critical rumination on the global nature of modernism, its possibilities, foibles, and its implications for culture as ways of living. Professor Mehta accepts the value of modernity but argues cogently and convincingly throughout for a rethinking of the foundations upon which it was built."

David Bell, Associate Professor,
School of Architecture, Rensselaer Polytechnic Institute

Critiquing the Modern in Architecture

JAIMINI MEHTA

Routledge
Taylor & Francis Group

NEW YORK AND LONDON

First published 2018
by Routledge
711 Third Avenue, New York, NY 10017

and by Routledge
2 Park Square, Milton Park, Abingdon, Oxon OX14 4RN

Routledge is an imprint of the Taylor & Francis Group, an informa business

Library of Congress Cataloguing in Publication Data
Names: Mehta, Jamini, author.
Title: Critiquing the modern in architecture / Jamini Mehta.
Description: New York : Routledge, 2018. | Includes bibliographical
    references and index.
Identifiers: LCCN 2017012690| ISBN 9781138690790 (hardback) | ISBN
    9781138690806 (pbk.) | ISBN 9781315536729 (master ebook) | ISBN
    9781134998784 (mobi/kindle)
Subjects: LCSH: Architecture, Modern—20th century. | Architecture,
    Modern—21st century.
Classification: LCC NA680 .M39 2018 | DDC 724/.7—dc23
LC record available at https://lccn.loc.gov/2017012690

ISBN: 978-1-138-69079-0 (hbk)
ISBN: 978-1-138-69080-6 (pbk)
ISBN: 978-1-315-53672-9 (ebk)

Typeset in Univers LT Std
by Swales & Willis Ltd, Exeter, Devon, UK

Contents

Acknowledgments

This book, though made up of essays written for disparate occasions and purposes, is in reality born from extended interactions with countless students and academic colleagues whose probing questions and curiosity have helped in clarifying my own often unformed thoughts. Thus, this book is for all those who have contributed in shaping it in more ways than I can list. Still, I must specifically acknowledge the following: the late professors Kurula Varkey at CEPT and Kenneth Warriner at RPI deserve special mention for being tough sounding boards. A few of my former students, who started out as students but invariably ended up as friends, I want to thank specifically (in alphabetical order). Anuradha Mathur, Rahul Mehrotra, Rajmohan Shetty and Snehal Nagarsheth were among those who started the journal *Akshara*, claimed my office as their editorial headquarters and came up with the most probing and provocative questions to always keep me on edge. Punita, who has remained with me as companion and partner for life, read many of my early drafts and made no-nonsense comments that always made them better.

Gautam Balsekar's study of social space and Vrinda Makwana (Pant), with her focused study of the Brihadeshwara temple, opened up avenues for looking at alternative conceptions of space. William Whitekar, Director of the Architectural Archives, University of Pennsylvania, provided the crucial archival material including press cuttings, correspondences and images for the essay on Giurgola. And finally, I am grateful to Wendy Fuller at Routledge who piloted my proposal through the rigorous process of scrutiny and review without ever losing faith.

Introduction

The Metaphysical Foundations of Modern Architecture

This book endeavors to explore the idea of the "modern" in architecture both in its theoretical as well as practical forms. The various essays in this collection were originally written over the last four decades, each in entirely different circumstances. Looking back on the 40 years of my own intellectual production I realized a persistent theme running through some of them: to understand the inherent contradictions of theoretical postulates that have informed modern architecture and its built production. This led to the selection of these essays here as a way to articulate a critique of the idea of the modern as we have largely inherited it through the so-called modern movement in architecture.

There is no dearth of literature on modern architecture. Since the beginning of the twentieth century, when a sense of the emergence of something new began to be felt, the architectural intelligentsia, especially in Europe and America, has been particularly prolific in outlining its profile and laying bare its multiple facets. By all accounts, it has been a robust and liberating phenomenon and has produced great architecture. Growing up, and being trained as an architect at a time when this movement was at its peak, one could not help but be carried away by its tsunami-like wave.

Still, there was always this nagging feeling that it did not quite accommodate, and was not responsive to, a rhythm of life, a pattern of habitation, an occupation of space and a relationship of humans with their external world that was born out of the experiences of people other than those of the Western civilization from where this idea of modernity had originated. But it claimed to be international and accorded universal attributes for all humankind. It was obvious to me that this contradiction was far more structural than superficial and needed to be explored by going down to the very metaphysical foundations on which this edifice of modern architecture is built.

The "modernity project"[1] seems to have begun with a series of events in Europe around the sixteenth and seventeenth centuries. The publication in 1543 of Copernicus's *On the Revolutions of the Celestial Spheres* and the availability of its empirical evidence in 1609 when Galileo was the first to point a telescope skyward, and finally in 1637 René Descartes' proclamation "I think, therefore I am" (*Cogito ergo sum*);[2] these are the major events which can be said to have engendered modernity. Both individually and collectively, these events pointed towards one of the most significant epistemological shifts in the history of

Western thought: the separation of body and mind. The Cartesian doubt that the senses may not be as reliable as we thought led to the faculty of reason acquiring a central position in the affairs of humans.

Thus modernity was aimed at transforming day-to-day life, until then structured around and determined by religion and traditional metaphysics, and putting it on a rational footing. Jurgen Habermas has described this as the

> separation of substantive reason expressed in religion and metaphysics into three autonomous spheres. They are science, morality and art. These came to be differentiated because the unified worldviews of religion and metaphysics fell apart. Since the eighteenth century, the problems inherited from these older worldviews could be arranged so as to fall under specific aspects of validity: truth, normative rightness, authenticity and beauty. . . . Each domain of culture could be made to correspond to cultural professions in which problems could be dealt with as the concern of special experts.[3]

Consolidated by the mid-seventeenth century, modernity can be characterized by a number of defining traits. These were secularization of culture, establishment of the autonomous individual, universalization, urbanism, acculturation of ideas and ahistoricism. This modernist movement was an all-encompassing paradigm shift involving a fundamental change in view of the world that began in Europe initially but spread fast to other parts of the world to various degrees. Many of us had accepted and assumed this to be an inevitable consequence of a continuous and ongoing historical process. We had also assumed its underlying rationale, the centrality of reason, as universally valid and equally applicable to all societies, cultures and civilizations globally. As Paul Ricoeur wrote in 1965,

> We have to keep in mind that if science is Greek in its origin and European through Galileo, Descartes, Newton, etc., science does not foster this power of unifying mankind because it is Greek or European but because it is a human dimension. It manifests a sort of *de jure* unity which controls all the other features of civilization . . . it is a purely abstract and rational unity of mankind which leads to all the other manifestations of modern civilization.[4]

These other manifestations of modern civilization include architecture. But the identity of modern architecture, as constructed to align it with modern science and industry, was unable to adequately explain architecture emerging from other parts of the world. It has been clear for some time now that modernism, so narrowly defined, has not lived up to its promise to represent the universal cultural modernity premised on an all-encompassing knowledge revolution. Other non-Western societies have developed different ways of seeing and making the environment which are equally valid and offer the critical foil to unravel the taken-for-granted assumptions of the dominant Western view of the world, and works done outside Europe have the potential to critique the claim of universal civilization. But a word of caution is called for here: this must not be formulated in terms of West versus the rest. Nor is it a question of arriving at a vague form of syncretism or fusion. This demands a recognition and acceptance of the plurality of multiple thought-worlds and that not all of these have accorded reason the same centrality as has the Western one.

That the binary of West and the East exists is not disputed. But does it then imply that the two streams of thought are like two banks of a river always remaining parallel, never meeting and more importantly, never fertilizing each other? Such a proposition must be rejected. There is ample historical evidence to establish that the seemingly autonomous metaphysical schemes of both Greek and Indian cultures have not only developed in parallel to each other but have also mutually influenced one another.[5] The differences are those of form and emphasis rather than that of analytic rigor. While the former culture follows a deductive method, the latter goes by an inductive and analogical method. One emphasizes reason and consciousness, the other dwells on perception and ontology.[6] These thought-worlds are not limited to philosophical inquiries and discourses but permeate all cultural life and mold people's sensibilities too. Aesthetic productions, including architecture, must then be viewed in this context. A truly universal architectural modernity can be built by distinguishing between the universality of reason and technology, both of which have no fixed domain, and architectural expressions that spring from a multitude of thought-worlds. We will then have a variety of simultaneous narratives of place making, formal configurations and forms of habitation, each appropriate to its situation, yet universal.

Still, this does open up the prospect of critically looking at one thought-world from the standpoint of another, that is, to sense the essential underlying structure of ideas and values of a thought tradition by viewing it from outside. This is the position I have taken. Paul Ricoeur, whom I have quoted above, has also made another observation:

> No one can say what will become of our civilization when it has really met different civilizations by means other than the shock of conquest and domination. But we have to admit that *this encounter has not yet taken place at the level of an authentic dialogue.*[7]
>
> (italics mine)

While the essays in this collection do not take an overtly critical stance, I am hopeful that readers will sense a certain commonality within these disparate texts, an alternative narrative, and an attempt to engage with other thought-worlds, running through all of them, more pronounced in some, less in others.

The essays are grouped in three parts. The first part, "Rethinking Modernity," explores and interrogates the metaphysical foundations of modernity in general and of modernism in architecture in particular. This critique takes off from the position that we live in multiple thought-worlds and that the roots of the dominant rationalist narrative go all the way down to the pre-Socratic Greek thoughts. A parallel and equally ancient universe of thought was developed by Indian and later by Arabic thinkers who considered intellect as a spiritual faculty capable of knowing and apprehending the reality in an unmediated fashion. While reason accesses knowledge through conceptual filtration, the intellect perceives it in a direct manner without the sequential mediation of thought and reasoning. This locates intellect in the ontological realm of forms and presences capable of being represented and symbolized in the physical world. Indeed this is one of the functions of Indian and Islamic architecture—to create a symbolic representation of the transience of this world and the greatness of the hereafter.

Each of these essays is an attempt to explore and understand an aspect of the idea of modernity and its manifestation in architecture whenever an occasion and an opportunity presented themselves before me and when it was appropriate to speak about this subject. Thus while the context may have determined the actual thematic focus, my own interest has found its way in, either directly or tangentially. Thus, this collection does not offer a singular and linear narrative wherein each chapter builds on from where the previous one left off. While each of the essays has a well-developed thematic consistency, the whole is more like a collage than a classical composition. This requires greater engagement from the reader to connect the various threads of the argument.

The decade of 1965–1975 was arguably one of the most eventful periods to be young in the United States and I happened to be there. The euphoria of humankind's first moon landing was soon eclipsed by student protests against the war in Vietnam in universities such as Kent State, Harvard and Columbia. I was teaching at Columbia where the students of architecture were questioning much more than the ethics of the war; in the words of Giancarlo De Carlo, they were questioning the very "purpose of their preparation."[8] It was hard to remain untouched by their intensity.

Thus, when I returned to India in 1975, I was immersed in this intensity and restlessness. Joining the School of Architecture, Ahmedabad (now CEPT University) to teach, I found myself mentoring a small group of equally restless students eager to know more about what was happening elsewhere. They had started a journal, *Akshara*, dedicated to explorations of ideas in architecture and invited me to contribute an essay. "Toward a Purposeful Disequilibrium" (Chapter 1 in this volume) was my reflection on the events of the preceding few years and also on the realization of the inadequacies of architectural thought we have inherited from the modern movement. Looking back at this essay after more than 30 years I was struck by its almost revolutionary fervor and a manifesto-like intensity. The staccato rhythm and the short sentences of the writing betrayed a state of mind and an urgency to address the built-in contradictions of the modernist thought in architecture prevalent at that time. I have slightly edited it for this compilation.

In 1983 I was invited to teach at Rensselaer Institute in Troy, New York. "A Fool's Paradise: A Critical Evaluation of the Sources of Post-Modern Architecture" (Chapter 2 in this volume) was a public lecture I gave there. It extends the arguments and concerns hinted at in the previous essay and explores the roots of what was then increasingly referred to as post-modern architecture. These concerns remain and can be seen as a subterranean attitude informing many of the essays in this collection. "Interrogative Scholarship: Theorizing the Agenda for Post-Rational Architecture" (Chapter 3 in this volume), written only about a year ago, attempts a possible bridge across the East–West binary, referred to above, by interrogating and taking a critical look at both these thought-worlds from each other's perspective. It has never been published before.

Throughout history the production of built architecture has happened parallel with the production of ideas about what architecture is or should be. It is in the schools of architecture that this interconnectedness is most visible. Thus, it is impossible to critique modernist thought without looking at its pedagogical consequences. Since the 1970s, schools throughout the world have been preoccupied with the task of realigning their pedagogies with the changing conditions of practice. "Contingent Criticality" (Chapter 4 in this volume) is an edited compilation of some of my presentations at a number of academic forums. Like the other three essays in this part, this too takes off from a position that, for any substantial epistemological course correction, the narrative will have to return to the root assumptions that have informed the modernist discourse. In other words, we need to rethink the very foundation on which we have built the edifice of modernity. These four essays are thus connected and may be read together.

The second group of essays, under the part title "The Idea of Architecture," resulted from my half a century's engagement with academics. Countless interactions with students and colleagues in various schools where I have taught, in India as well as elsewhere, have raised a number of questions regarding the nature of the activity we call architecture. Every building, like every work of art, embodies ideas that transcend the moment of its creation and the personal situation of its architect. It tells of the intellectual and material cultures which engender it. An architect, more often than not, internalizes these and they, in turn, get expressed through his/her choices. It is in academia that these ideas are discussed, deliberated and analyzed to push the boundaries of the profession. Teaching, for me, has always been a site for creative thinking. Often the work of a student, although focused on a specific and concrete situation, prompts one to question some longstanding and taken-for-granted assumptions. A casual question by another sometimes takes one into unexplored areas. The cumulative results of these encounters are the births of ideas that may not always be new but that always reveal something about me to myself. These I have articulated at various times either as lectures or parts of graduate seminars. The four essays in this part address this; some directly and others tangentially.

"Architecture and the Idea of Agreement" (Chapter 5 in this volume) was an annual lecture delivered at CEPT University, Ahmedabad in 2013 in memory of my friend and architect Prof. Kurula Varkey. It was aimed at drawing the attention of the academic community to those timeless values of architecture which transcend the exigencies and the debates of the moment and restate what I refer to as *the idea of architecture*. The two essays, "The Space of Mr. Giedion" and "Architecture as Co-Making" (Chapters 6 and 7 in this volume) came about through my notes for a graduate seminar course I had devised and conducted in several schools in India, between 2003 and 2012. They interrogate the concept of space so central to the twentieth-century architectural discourse.

When confronted with a task to design something, we architects often furiously sketch to clear our heads of the cobwebs of ideas and images until we arrive at some clarity about what it is that we are searching for. I also write to clear my head when I find myself confronted with a question that is not resolved. The essay "*Vaastu* and the Enfolding Order" (Chapter 8 in this volume) happened this way. During my numerous engagements with students, I had not been able to deal satisfactorily with questions raised by them to explain the mysteries of *Vaastu Shastra*, the ancient Indian wisdom on architecture. And that had been nagging me. Unfortunately, there has not been much debate on the subject and the present practitioners often project it as a dogma with set rituals. What I have presented here for the first time should not be taken as a definitive interpretation or explanation of the ancient texts. However, it provided an opportunity to look at ancient wisdom from the perspective of Western rationalism and vice versa. It is an approach, a reasonable intellectual position which may spark an informed debate. I will be happy if that happens.

The essays in the third part, "On Praxis," are critical explorations of modernist practice through specific works of architects. When invited to speak on the work of an architect in the context of an event or a publication to celebrate their work, I have often used these occasions to view the work from a perspective that was of interest to me at that time, which is to articulate a critique of the modernist ideas. This set of essays complements the one before it, one addressing the metaphysical foundation and the other the actual practice of architecture. Still, it is not necessary to read these essays in any particular order.

"Le Corbusier: Polemical, Poetical and Existential" (Chapter 9 in this volume) was first presented at a symposium held to coincide with an exhibition of the master's work in Ahmedabad in 2007. I was already working on a project to find a way to talk about some of Corbu's works outside of his vocabulary of *L'esprit Nouveau*. There was a nagging feeling that the modernist polemics which accompanied much of Corbu's career cannot satisfactorily explain some of his works such as the chapel at Ronchamp and the monastery at La Tourette, and needed a different approach. The symposium was the platform for putting this to the test in front of a knowledgeable group of architects.

Similarly, "Analogs of Architecture" (Chapter 10 in this volume) was commissioned for and published in a catalog of an exhibition of models made in the atelier of architect Balkrishna Doshi in 2003. The exhibition prompted me to think about an area of our work which we routinely engage in but rarely pay serious attention to as a crucial element of, and an instrument in, the process of designing. Models, as three-dimensional analogs of the eventual architecture, seemed far more crucial in this process than merely as part of the presentation. The exhibition of Doshi's models provided an opportunity to focus my as yet unfocused thoughts onto some kind of resolution.

I have been fortunate and privileged to be close to two of the masters of contemporary architecture: Louis I. Khan and Romaldo Giurgola, both members of what came to be known as the Philadelphia School. In 2011, I was asked to speak on the professional relationship between the two at a symposium celebrating the 90th birthday of Romaldo Giurgola at the University of Melbourne. This was the excuse to write "Romaldo Giurgola: The Reluctant Master" (Chapter 11 in this volume). My long association with Giurgola from 1965 to 1975, both as his associate and as a co-author, had given me a sense that his early work in the 1960s constituted a serious critique of the taken-for-granted conventional wisdom of modernism. The symposium in Melbourne was an opportunity to develop this sense into a coherent argument.

While in Melbourne, I had the opportunity to see the beautifully mounted exhibition on "Vienna Art and Design." Seeing all this work together provoked me to investigate it more, and this resulted in the last essay "The Vienna Spring" (Chapter 12 in this volume).

Like the other three previous praxes, this too seems to have touched the vein of what can be called the "Architecture of Resistance." And interestingly, all four answer to at least some of the qualities Kenneth Frampton has enumerated in his essay "Towards a Critical Regionalism: Six Points for an Architecture of Resistance."[9] Frampton, following Paul Ricoeur, has made a distinction between universal civilization, a desirable goal founded on reason, science and technical invention, all of which have "no fixed domain,"[10] and the multitude of cultures, spread around the globe, which are all the other manifestations of modern civilization with their own peculiarities. Frampton writes, "The fundamental strategy of Critical Regionalism is to *mediate* the impact of universal civilization with elements derived indirectly from the peculiarities of a particular place"[11] (emphasis mine).

I find this problematic on two counts. One, the idea of Critical Regionalism, a new direction for architecture, or as Fredric Jameson has described as a "belated form of modernism,"[12] so constructed, still clings onto the notion of a singular, syncretic universal civilization in whose metaphysical roots lay the centrality of reason precluding the possibility of a plurality of thought-worlds with their own "ethical and mythical nucleus."[13] That also precludes the encounter and the authentic dialog that Ricoeur was hoping for. And two, this is not about geography. The thought-worlds transcend the physicality of location and may even co-exist in nascent form at the threshold of change. After all, Le Corbusier, one of the finest polemicists of the universal civilization, was simultaneously exploring supposedly non-rational and experiential qualities in architecture. And so were the Vienna architects. Giurgola was clearly cultivating the site in search of the secular spirituality of the place, so alien to the regional culture of the West. In Chapter 7, I reveal similarities between thousand-year-old events in India and Nepal and the US pavilion at the Montreal World's Fair of 1967, establishing connections in both time and space. All betray the possibilities of that authentic dialog across the thought-worlds.

All cultures and societies have deep-rooted traditions, which include not only corporeal forms of architecture but also the grounds of beliefs and values to which these forms are rooted. The answer to these two problems then, lies not in mediating the impact of universal civilization with elements derived indirectly from the peculiarities of a particular place, as Frampton proposes, nor in "transfers and transformations" of elements taken from our dictionary of forms, as Charles Correa suggested.[14] It must be found by framing the discourse in terms of the dialectics of traditions and modernity and asking how we can define modernity within the context of those traditions which are still valid, and varied from culture to culture, and at the same time reinterpret those traditions in light of our desire to be modern, which is universal. Such a discourse was foreclosed when the "International Style" was declared to be the appropriate language for modern architecture.

Frampton does suggest the possibility of a "self-conscious synthesis between universal civilization and world culture," giving an illustration of Jørn Utzon's Bagsvaerd Church (1976). He interprets that the "*rationality* of normative technique" is represented here by the regular grid and the repetitive, in-fill modules and the "*arationality* of idiosyncratic form" is suggested by the highly configured section of the reinforced concrete vault inside, suggestive of the Chinese pagoda roof, picked out from the architect's memory bank of world architecture. I believe the issue of rationality goes beyond a regular grid or repetitive elements, and that the corporeal form, far from being arbitrarily idiosyncratic, must be rooted in the time and the place of its making, that is, its locality and its thought-world.

I have been experimenting with this issue with our own work and want to illustrate this with the example of a small suburban house, Villa Visaria (1982) in Ahmedabad, India (Figure 0.1). Universal rationality is embodied in the very form of the plan—the *plan-form*. It not only embraces the order of measure and ratios but also looks, in multiple ways, at the rational and thoughtful organization of space and elements that is appropriate not only to the specific program but also to the specificity of the locality. The language of corporeal forms (Figure 0.2), on the other hand, is true to locally available technology and craftsmanship. But this is achieved in a contemporary way as opposed to the "transfers and transformations" of traditional elements as suggested by Correa.

Only an acceptance of multiple thought-worlds with their own ethical and mythical nuclei, and a constant and ongoing dialog across them, can produce a truly universal modernity in architecture. The essays in this collection are aimed at initiating such a dialog.

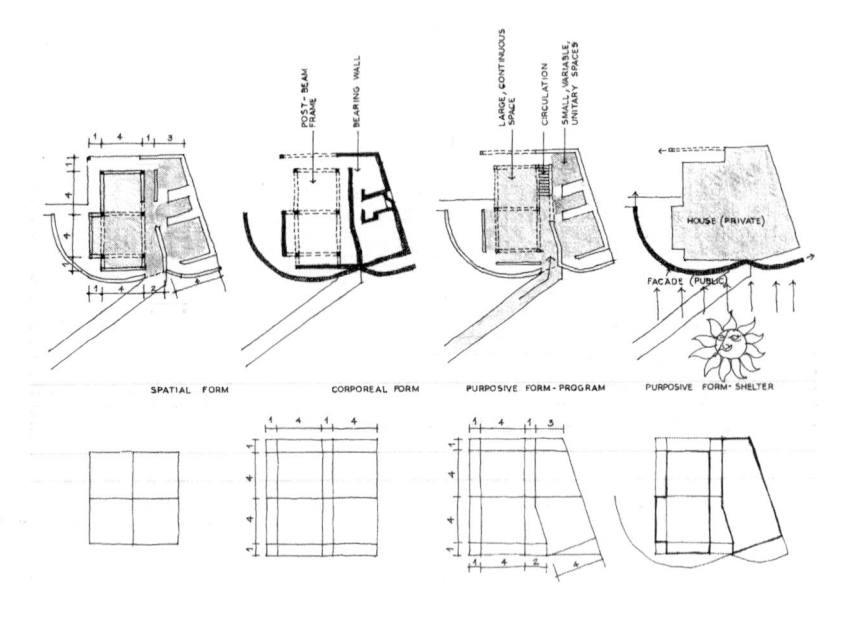

Figure 0.1
Plan-form.
Villa Visaria,
Ahmedabad,
Studio Jaimini
Mehta, 1982.

Figure 0.2
**Mask wall.
Villa Visaria,
Ahmedabad,
Studio Jaimini
Mehta, 1982.**

Notes

1 Jurgen Habermas. "Modernity: An Incomplete Project." In *The Anti-Aesthetic: Essays on Postmodern Culture*, ed. Hal Foster (Seattle: Bay Press, 1983), 3–15.

2 René Descartes. *Principles of Philosophy* (1644), Part 1, article 7. This proposition became a fundamental pillar of Western philosophy. It establishes self as a thinking entity whose existence cannot be doubled while it doubts (thinks).

3 Jurgen Habermas, ibid., 9.

4 Paul Ricoeur, "Universal Civilization and National Cultures." In *History and Truth*, trans. Charles A. Kelbley (Evanston: Northwestern University Press, 1965), 271–272.

5 Thomas McEvilley, *The Shape of Ancient Thought* (New York: Allworth Press, 2002).

6 Ibid., 511.

7 Paul Ricoeur, op. cit., 283.

8 Giancarlo De Carlo, "Legitimizing Architecture," *Forum*, 23(1) (1972), 9.

9 Kenneth Frampton, "Towards a Critical Regionalism: Six Points for an Architecture of Resistance." In *The Anti-Aesthetic: Essays on Postmodern Culture*, ed. Hal Foster (Seattle: Bay Press, 1983), 21.

10 Paul Ricoeur, op. cit., 272.

11 Kenneth Frampton, op. cit., 21.

12 Fredric Jameson, "The Constraints of Postmodernism." In *Rethinking Architecture: A Reader in Cultural Theory*, ed. N. Leach (London: Routledge, 1997), 235.

13 Paul Ricoeur, op. cit., 278.

14 Charles Correa, "Transfers and Transformations." In *Charles Correa* (Singapore: Concept Media Ltd., 1987), 165–175.

Part One
Rethinking Modernity

Chapter 1

Toward a Purposeful Disequilibrium

In the last years of the 1970s, the phenomenon of the "End of Ideology"[1] was nowhere more evident than in architecture. The intensity with which the programs and manifestos of the late nineteenth and early twentieth centuries were projected seems to have given way to a sobriety bordering on depression. The promise of an objective architecture has not materialized and architecture's ability to be a harbinger of a new order is beginning to look like an illusion.

Reactions to this vary depending upon one's own temperament and the interests one serves. The young and the radicals bemoan this ideological vacuum and reject or suspend architecture as part of bourgeois culture (the futility of which was beautifully expressed in the 1972 film by Luis Buñuel, *The Discreet Charm of the Bourgeoisie*), just as they reject or suspend its literature, its philosophy, or for that matter any activity that does not spark action or does not noticeably help in changing the world.

On the other hand, the conservatives in the grove of academe gleefully proclaim "we told you so." For them architecture begins and ends in the problem of ventilation and in the rising cost of land. They accept the corporate reality and the reality of the marketplace. Ironically—and this only sharpens the ideological confusion in architecture—both of these groups deny the distance and dissociation of architecture from life, albeit for very different reasons. If architecture is still anything at all, they say, it must be real and a part and parcel of life. While for the conservatives life represents the prevalent and established values, for the radicals life itself is a "conscious negation of the established way of life, with all its institutions, with its entire material and intellectual culture and its entire immoral morality."[2] This is increasingly being expressed by violating the supposed integrity, primacy and assumed inapproachability of the architectural object (Figure 1.1).

Examining the current crisis and its polemics, we observe that the present fissures in the ideological system of architecture may be the result of a built-in contradiction, the beginning of which can be traced to mid-nineteenth century. The nineteenth-century demand for structural and utilitarian integrity, initially thought to depend on the technical innovations of the Industrial Revolution, was in reality based more on the fundamental Cartesian revolution of thought itself. This utilitarianism reduced the object of architecture to that of an artifact of use. As Hannah Arendt has observed,

Figure 1.1
Negation of the integrity of the architectural object.

> the perplexity of utilitarianism is that it gets caught in the unending chain of means and ends without ever arriving at some principle which could justify the category of means and end, that is, of utility itself . . . in other words, utility established as meaning generates meaninglessness.[3]

Architecture thus got placed on a far lower level in the "hierarchy of organizations"[4] and became analogous to "clockwork."[5] Even after allowing for a degree of *cloudiness* in a clockwork system, it is safe to say that this is the level of predetermined dynamic structures repeating their movements because of some simple law of connectedness among their parts (Figure 1.2). Designing at this level implied a method involving (a) analysis of the nature of components and (b) their reconstitution into a problem-solving whole. This is precisely what Le Corbusier did at Unité d'Habitation at Marseille. He deconstructed the elements of habitation and reconstituted them in a new language (Figure 1.3). This was understood in both its material and conceptual sense.

But architecture is a cultural construct and when you extend the above argument to cultures, it implies a discontinuity between the classes of objects or institutions within a given culture, which usually demand to be treated in terms

Figure 1.2
Jens Olsen's astronomical clock in Copenhagen City Hall. Copenhagen, Denmark.

Figure 1.3
Components of habitat are deconstructed and then reconfigured in a new form. Le Corbusier, Unité d'Habitation, Marseille, France, 1952.

of their interdependency as, under stable conditions, they spring from the same core values (Figure 1.4) and are interdependent. The discontinuity implied by the machine metaphor, on the other hand, will have to be founded on an assumption that architecture has validity independent of its cultural context and is derived essentially from its own technologically determined history. We find it hard to accept this.

Thus divorced from its traditional cognitive role as a superstructure of society, no more governed by the same rules which govern other cultural manifestations, architecture came to rely more and more on the initial Kantian assumption that all concepts, even the questions posed in pure reason, reside not in experience but in the faculty of reason. It is reason that engendered these ideas. It followed that only the radical discontinuity between the reality of lived experience and the reality as knowable guarantees precision, objectivity and scientific accuracy (Figure 1.5). In science the use of experiments for the purpose of knowledge was already the consequence of the conviction that one can know only what one has made oneself. The much discussed shift of emphasis in the history of architecture, from the old question of "what" or "why" to the new question of "how" is a direct consequence of this conviction.

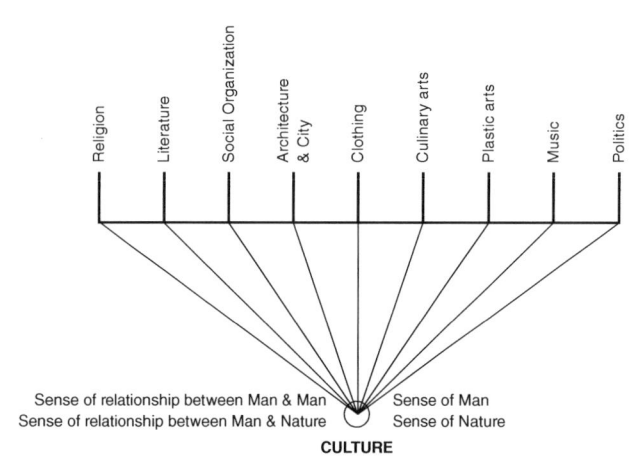

Religion | Literature | Social Organization | Architecture & City | Clothing | Culinary arts | Plastic arts | Music | Politics

Sense of relationship between Man & Man — Sense of Man
Sense of relationship between Man & Nature — Sense of Nature

CULTURE

Figure 1.4
Superstructural manifestations of culture. In a stable cultural milieu, all visible expressions spring from the same set of beliefs and values.

Figure 1.5
"Systema solare et planetarium." The primacy of reason. Perceived geocentricity is replaced by a new rational order. In this illustration by Johann Doppelmayr, Athena is shown preferring the new sun-centric universe. Nuremberg, Germany, 1742.

Thus from an analysis of *process* there emerged a discipline of formal composition which symbolized process itself (Figure 1.6).

> In place of the concept of being, we now find the concept of becoming (process). And whereas it is in the nature of being to appear and thus disclose itself, it is in the nature of process to remain invisible, to be something whose existence can only be inferred from the presence of certain phenomena.[6]

However, in order to make process visible in architecture it was necessary to reduce the object of architecture further as a commodity of consumption. In a series of graphic representations of hypothetical projects, the British avant-garde group Archigram, not unlike the Japanese Metabolism, projected an architecture whose language was derived from the natural processes of change and growth. Architecture thus derived its validity to the extent that it was a representation of this natural process. For only by being a part of the never-ending natural process of humankind's metabolism with nature, by acquiring an exchange value in the cycle of consumption and regeneration and by reverting back to the realm of nature can architecture symbolize process. The fact that the desire for universality in architecture can only be fulfilled at the cost of putting a decisive distance between people as *humans* and their built environment is the built-in contradiction mentioned earlier.

Simultaneous to this domination of "how" over "what" is also the domination of *functional ideology* over ideology as *secular religion*. The distinction is significant since the much proclaimed "end of ideology" may actually be a replacement of an all-inclusive system of comprehensive reality, a set of beliefs, infused with passion, which seeks to transform the whole way of life, with an ideology which has "the social function of maintaining the overall structure of society by inducing men to accept in their consciousness, the place and the role assigned to them by this structure"[7] (Figure 1.7). In other words, an ideology with an agenda.

Figure 1.6
Process of change is the determinant of formal language. Nakagin Capsule Tower, Kisho Kurokawa.

Figure 1.7
Toward a rational architecture. The muse of architecture is pointing toward a primitive model of the bare essential elements. Illustration by Charles Dominique Joseph Eisen, 1755.

Thus the *architect as a person* had to be divorced from the *architect as a professional*. As the former they can be a force *in* society while as the latter they can only be a force *of* society. The implications of all this are quite direct. For one, a rational analysis of architecture alone is inadequate. What people say they believe cannot always be taken at face value, and one must search for the structure of interest beneath the ideas; one looks not at the content of theories but at their functions.[8]

A second, more radical conclusion is that if ideas mask material interests, then the truth of the doctrine is linked with the interest it serves. Thus in the present situation, there seems to be no objective architecture, only *bourgeois architecture* and *proletarian architecture*, or high architecture and low architecture. One is expected to take sides. The alternative is to take refuge in the dispassionate professionalism of singling out one value without linking it to others.

The point here is that the "end of ideology," far from being a historical necessity, is one of the unintended byproducts of modernism, the direct consequence of which is to make architecture irrelevant by its failure to represent public ideas. For the relevance of architecture lies not in its ability to satisfy the exigencies of the moment, but in its ability to project the image of a just and humane society.

But slogans can be over-simplistic and may even be taken as alibi for inaction. In order to avoid this, it is necessary to clarify here the dialectical relation between architecture and its social context.

Every society is characterized by the way it organizes the life of its members. This involves an initial choice between alternatives, which are determined by the initial level of the material and the intellectual culture. It is a determinate choice involving the seizure of one among other ways of comprehending, organizing and transforming reality.

While in the traditional, and more stable societies there existed, in the initial choice, a reciprocity of perspective whereby architecture and society mirror each other,[9] this reciprocity is far more complex in societies in which the various manifestations of culture may be linked with different value systems—cultural data—which themselves may be constantly shifting (Figure 1.8). Thus art in societies under transformation is bound to present a thoroughly confusing picture of overlapping and contrasting value systems. This was tellingly represented by Charlie Chaplin in his 1936 film *Modern Times*. In an iconic sequence, the protagonist, simply referred to as the Factory Worker, is shown in front of, and holding with both hands, parts of a large machine, which he does not understand. The machine represents that part of the culture which has clearly shifted the datum and this disconnect is visible in the bewildered gaze of the man, who still exists on the old datum.

Whereas all substantial changes in social structure—shifts in cultural data—create their own tangible symbols in architecture, the formation of a conceptual system on the social level is a precondition for its manifestation on the physical level.

On the other hand, for these transformations to become cognizant, they must first be concretized in architecture. Thus architecture is unique among all the superstructural activities such as language, myth, social organization and so on, in that it is at once both a consequence and a cause of social change. Reflecting on Claes Oldenburg's proposal to erect a giant monument, in the shape of a peeled banana, in Times Square (Figure 1.9), Herbert Marcuse observed that these works can be a bloodless means to achieve radical change, and went on to predict that such a sculpture might bring on a revolution because, "then people cannot take anything seriously; neither their President, nor the Cabinet, nor the corporation executives."[10] Architecture thus has the advantage of being able to project ahead through concrete images, through physically perceptible events, the physical environment of a society built on a different set of values: Oldenburg has elevated trivia to the level of profound. What is suggested here is not the omnipotence of architecture which can lead to fantastic and unrealistic schemes alienated from the social space. Far from it, what we want to point out is the cognitive role of architecture which may be *alienating* without being *alienated*.

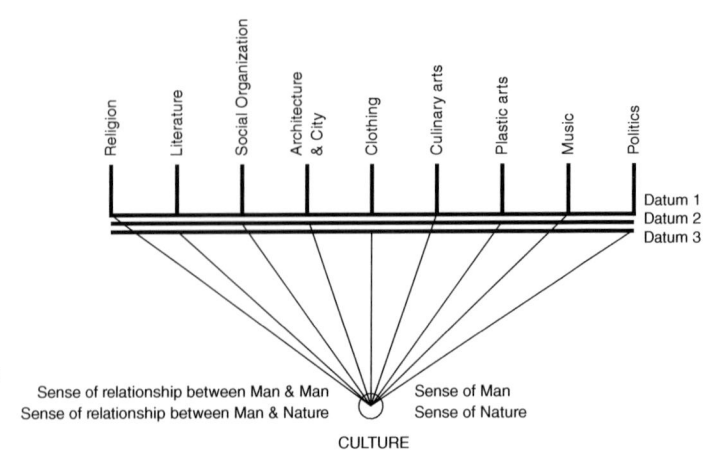

Figure 1.8
Superstructural manifestations of a culture in transition. All visible expressions are not aligned to the same datum and are likely to result in a mismatch.

Religion · Literature · Social Organization · Architecture & City · Clothing · Culinary arts · Plastic arts · Music · Politics

Datum 1
Datum 2
Datum 3

Sense of relationship between Man & Man
Sense of relationship between Man & Nature
Sense of Man
Sense of Nature

CULTURE

Figure 1.9
Proposal for a peeled banana monument in the middle of Times Square. Claes Oldenberg, 1969.

A possible method emerges from the above which is diametrically opposed to the method employed by science. In other words, the relationship between "events" (percepts) and "structures" (concepts), to borrow from Lévi-Strauss,[11] is reversed in architecture to that in science. While science seeks to create events and objects (technological transformations) through conceptual structures, architecture seeks to create structures of cognition through a set of events and objects (which may include those left behind by the shifting cultural datum). The *initial choice* defines the range of possible ways in which these events and objects may be combined, and precludes alternative possibilities incompatible with it.

Thus architecture is part of an established culture to the extent that it derives its raw material from it. As such it is an affirmative force sustaining this culture: a force *of* the society. It is alienating to the extent that it proposes an alternative to the established reality. In that sense it is a force *in* the society and a negating force. The harmonization of this antagonism provides the essential tension in architecture.

The nature of architecture depends, then, not upon the nature of the individual events (signs)[12] that compose it, but on the relationships between a number of contemporary cultural constructs which elevate these events into meaningful structures. The activity is analogous to myth-making in pre-rational societies in the sense that it is indeed relating or ordering differences into a structure that confers interest or value upon signs.

Revealed here is the extraordinary propensity of the human mind not only to organize, through sign systems, its experience of the world, but also in the process to reveal the threshold of the human; that level at which people passing from nature to culture become *human*.

Having identified the metaphysical sources of modern architecture and the various ideological detours resulting in the present devaluation of its objective, we have noted that this devaluation is the result of the method and logic of science being carried and applied in architecture. But we know that the limitation inherent in the method of observation and communication limits the phenomenon to be observed and communicated.[13] This limitation concerns our notion of the real, initiated in the philosophy of the seventeenth century. Moving toward abstraction it seeks its aesthetic validity from within, in a diachronic development of its formal vocabulary in time, negating any role played by other cultural manifestations.

On the social and urban level, it concerns our notion of the private and public domains and the line of demarcation in between. One of the most intriguing paradoxes of our time is that, while the technological resources for more complex social and urban structures such as buildings, transport and communication systems increase, we find a gradual simplification of social interactions and forms of social exchange.[14]

Civilizations the world over have always distinguished the family and the city as two distinct domains. This distinction is gradually being lost with the family increasingly appropriating the social functions and contacts that humans once sought in the broader arena of the city. The simplification of social space implies not only the gradual isolation and intensification of the family, but also the fact that the world between humans has lost its power to gather them together, to relate and to separate them and make them aware of the presence of others. Alberto Giacometti succinctly expresses this essential loneliness of modern humans (Figure 1.10).

According to Greek thought, the human capacity for political organization is not only different from but stands in direct opposition to that natural association

Figure 1.10
Alberto Giacometti's figures express the essential loneliness of modern humans. Alberto Giacometti, 1901–1966.

Figure 1.11
Modern infrastructure constitutes the technical apparatus of production and distribution. It also determines desires and aspirations. In doing so, it transcends its instrumentality.

whose center is the home and the family. Hannah Arendt has pointed out that "it was not just an opinion or theory of Aristotle but a simple historical fact that the foundation of the polis was preceded by the destruction of all organized units resting on kinship."[15]

But in an advanced industrial society, in which the technical apparatus of production and distribution (Figure 1.11) do not function merely as the sum-total of mere instruments which can be isolated from their social and political effects, such apparatus constitutes a system which determines a priori the product of the apparatus as well as the operations of servicing and extending it. In this form it tends to become totalitarian to the extent to which it determines not only the socially needed occupations, skills and attitudes, but also individual needs and aspirations. This happens when an object of use, such as a car or a cell phone, turns into an object of desire. Advertising glorifies the exchange value of commodities. To paraphrase Walter Benjamin, it creates a framework in which their use-value recedes into the background to be replaced by a kind of "sex appeal of the inorganic."[16] This obliterates the opposition between the private and the public existence, between individual and social needs.[17]

This distinction between the private and the public spheres of life, corresponding to the household and the political realms, which have existed as distinct, separate entities at least since the rise of the ancient city-state, has not only gradually disappeared, but the private has replaced the public. Architecture, an inherently public art, found itself relegated to the private realm when its object was reduced to the level of a commodity of consumption, whose durability is linked to the transience of test. It is worth recalling the words of Hannah Arendt:

> Without taking things out of nature's hand and consuming them, and without defending himself against the natural processes of growth and decay, the *animal laborans* could never survive. But without being at home in the midst of things whose durability makes them fit for use and for erecting a world whose very permanence stands in direct contrast to life, this life would never be human.[18]

The foregoing suggests that a radical reversal of values is a prerequisite to generating the necessary conceptual and methodological tools for an architecture we would like to call pro-human. The authentic architecture of the future will not be created by those who desperately try to produce the absence of form and a union with real life, but rather by those who do not recoil from the exigencies of form.

This form will be evident not in the corporeal properties of certain objects (*objets d'art*), but as forms and modes of existence corresponding to the reason and sensibilities of free individuals who will be judged by their actions in the public arena. It will be evident not in parts isolated from their environment, but in the internal organization which lends meaning to parts and, in the process, suggests new and unpredictable patterns of human relationships. It will be evident not in rigid order, fear of change and a desire for sameness, but in anarchy and disorder,[19] constant change and diversity.

It will be evident not in an economically stratified society manifesting in low-, middle- or upper-income housing estates (an inherently repressive and exploitative system), but in an architecture whose formal validity will have been linked with the timeless desires of humans, free of such fragmentations.

And it will be evident in a qualitatively different society in which a new type of people, no longer the subject or object of exploitation, can develop, in their life and work, the vision of the suppressed aesthetic possibilities of humans and things.

It will take a long time for this to happen. But, to paraphrase Arthur Rimbaud,[20] only with burning patience can we conquer the Splendid City which will give light, justice and dignity to all humankind.

Notes

1 Daniel Bell, *The End of Ideology* (New York: The Free Press, 1965).
2 Herbert Marcuse, "Art as a Form of Reality." In *On the Future of Art*, ed. Edward F. Fry (New York: The Viking Press, 1970), 123–134.
3 Hannah Arendt, *The Human Condition* (Chicago: University of Chicago Press, 1958), 154.
4 Ludwig von Bertalanffy, *General System Theory* (New York: George Braziller, 1968).
5 Karl R. Popper, "Of Clouds and Clocks." In *Objective Knowledge. An Evolutionary Approach* (London: Oxford University Press, 1972), 206–255.
6 Hannah Arendt, op. cit., 296–297.
7 Diana Agrest and Mario Gandelsonas, "Semiotics and Architecture: Ideological Consumption or Theoretical Work," *Opposition*, 1 (Sept. 1973), 94.
8 I have elaborated this point in my book, *Rethinking Modernity* (New Delhi: Niyogi Books, 2011).
9 Anthropologist Claude Lévi-Strauss has demonstrated that this reciprocity is manifest in the way the Bororo tribes, inhabiting the Amazon rainforest, lay out their villages in a circular form representing their cosmology. All the Christian missionaries had to do to convert them was to lay the village in the square form. This effectively disoriented them by shifting their anchor. Claude Lévi-Strauss, *Structural Anthropology* (New York: Anchor Books, 1967).

10 Quoted in Beth Py-Lieberman, "The Really Big Art of Claes Oldenburg," *Smithsonian Magazine* (Aug. 1995), available at: www.smithsonianmag.com/arts-culture/the-really-big-art-of-claes-oldenburg-1-35271235/.

11 Claude Lévi-Strauss, *The Savage Mind* (Chicago: University of Chicago Press, 1966).

12 I try to follow here Ferdinand de Saussure's definition of "sign" (the units of the system) as a double entity composed of the "signifier" and the "signified". Following this, signification is defined as a relation, internal to the sign, linking the signifier and signified. Saussure shows that signification is essentially arbitrary and is determined by an external relation which he calls value. Ferdinand de Saussure, *Course in General Linguistics* (New York: McGraw-Hill, 1966).

13 Werner Heisenberg, *Physics and Beyond* (New York: Harper & Row, 1971).

14 Richard Sennett, *The Uses of Disorder: Personal Identity and City Life* (New York: Vintage Books, 1970), 51.

15 Hannah Arendt, op. cit., 24.

16 Walter Benjamin, "Paris: Capital of the Nineteenth Century," *Perspecta*, 12 (1969), 163–172.

17 Herbert Marcuse, *One-Dimensional Man, Studies in the Ideology of Advanced Industrial Society* (Boston: Beacon Press, 1968), xv.

18 Hannah Arendt, op. cit., 135.

19 I am using these terms in the sense that Richard Sennett uses them in *Uses of Disorder*. With a provocative argument Sennett shows that unlike popular and conventional wisdom, anarchy and disorder can have a positive value.

20 Arthur Rimbaud, *A Season in Hell*, April–Aug. 1873.

Chapter 2

A Fool's Paradise

A Critical Evaluation of the Sources of Post-Modern Architecture

When I was a young student of architecture in the early 1960s, we were given two *mantras* by which to guide our work. One was *form follows function*, which referred to the seemingly inevitable causality between the formal resolution of a building and the utilitarian activities that it contains, one following the other like a shadow. The second was the equally inevitable equality between a house and machine: we were told that a house is simply a machine to live in. These were the two received wisdoms with which we entered the profession of architecture.

These were not simple statements of facts or instructions to young architects to help them find their future direction. These were slogans and, like all slogans, ideologically loaded. By elevating technology to the level of ideology and by making a building form valid only to the extent of its capacity to contribute positively to the activities it contains, the authors of these slogans were projecting a new classification of the external environment; a classification predicated upon the values of efficiency, universality and the linear progression of history— all basic, primary tenets of Cartesian/Kantian rationalism. During these past two centuries, these values have become so implanted in our minds that we have begun to think of them as eternal values: efficiency in terms of a ratio describing a relation between the efforts spent and the benefits gained; universality in terms of the capacity of the human endeavor, including architecture, to transcend culturally gained identities and be universally applicable—which reduces all cultural values to frivolity; and linearity of history implying a direction and aim of all human endeavor towards a utopia founded with the most efficient and the most universal elements; in other words, a "Universal Civilization" as elaborated by Paul Ricoeur.[1]

Now, architecture is a mode of knowledge, a way to conceptualize and internalize the external world. In other words, it is a system by which the external world, both animate as well as inanimate, consisting of things as well as relationships, with all its multitude of information, is classified and made knowledgeable into comprehensible categories by the way we organize our built environment. The criteria of this classification are provided by culturally accepted norms and values at any given time. Thus, through the ideas and method implicit in those slogans architecture was to concretize, and thus make cognizant the ideas and values which were dominant at that time, but had their origin in Cartesian Rationalism.

The Cartesian apprehension of the reality of lived experience subtly eroded and undermined the traditional object of architecture as a discursive activity throughout the eighteenth and nineteenth centuries. This was an apprehension not only of perceptible appearances but also of an intuitive sensing of the essence of being. It ended up in the early twentieth century as merely a mode of building predicated on the precepts of economically determined functionalism, the metaphor for which was to be the proverbial machine.

As Walter Benjamin observed in 1928, every epoch dreams about the epoch that is to succeed it. However, and paradoxically, there are always elements of utopia, of prehistoric classless society, drawn from the collective unconscious, which find their expression in forms ranging from ephemeral fashions to architecture. Fourier's Phalanstery was one such expression whose origin can be attributed to the appearance of machines.

The Phalanstery was to lead men back into relations in which morality would become superfluous. Its highly complicated organization resembled machinery. This machinery, formed of men, produced the land of Cockaigne, the primal wish symbol that Fourier's Utopia had filled with new life [Figure 2.1].[2]

Thus machines, those steamships and cooling towers, not only provided new forms to enrich architecture but also provided the analogy, an active metaphor, with which architecture was to express, in sensuous forms, a new classification, a reorganization of society based on the values of efficiency, universality and progress. So overwhelming and so powerful was the inspiration of the machine that it did not occur to the authors of the new slogans that this entailed a far more fundamental change, a shift in the conceptual system of architecture and not merely a substitution of new symbols for the old. The use of the machine as a metaphor

Figure 2.1 **Fourier's Phalanstery was a gigantic building housing a cooperative commune of 400 families engaged in agricultural activities. Illustration by Charles-François Daubigny.**

in architecture presupposes a method of designing which involves (a) splitting an architectural entity into its various components, (b) analysis of the nature of these components independent of each other and (c) their reconstitution as a problem-solving whole (Figure 1.3).

The fact that the architectural implications of such a method were not obvious in the beginning is understandable. The nineteenth century had not only been the age of technology and of what Carlyle sarcastically called *Victorious Analysis*,[3] it had also been the century in which science supposed it had established its intellectual foundations. This was when the method of science was the manipulation of exact measurements and when the philosophy implied by that method—the philosophy that took not only the components of physical entity but also matter and mind as independently existing substances—was the philosophy of scientific materialism and determinism. It was Lord Kelvin who proclaimed the faith which scientists have long since renounced although, alas, it has still remained as the credo of some members of our own profession:

> when you can measure what you are speaking about, and express it in numbers, you know something about it; but when you cannot measure it, when you cannot express it in numbers, your knowledge is of a meager and unsatisfactory kind; . . . you have scarcely in your thoughts advanced to the state of Science.[4]

Science, in other words, came to be admired as the puritan guardian of literal truth, whose aim it was to describe the material world visibly to the last decimal point.

Analysis presupposes a discontinuity, a separation, between a series of activities within a given culture, which usually demand to be treated in terms of their formal co-existence and interdependence. In other words, the various superstructural manifestations of a culture, such as architecture, literature, philosophy, technology, religion, mythology and so on all have a relationship of interdependency and are complete or make sense only to the extent that they are rooted to the same set of values (Figure 1.4). But the acceptance of analytical methods as a way to study cultural phenomena presupposes that all these activities be treated as component parts of the culture and can be separated from the totality and contemplated independently. It also implies that they can be studied only on the basis of certain universally applicable categories. Thus architecture, which unlike other activities has an objective presence, came more and more to be studied on the basis of certain visual qualities of the object and its instrumentality, that is, its capacity to serve utilitarian ends. Once alienated from its cultural context, architecture can only be justified by criteria from within, that is to say from its own history and its morphological evolution.

The categories of efficiency, universality and preoccupation with history not only presuppose each other but are also inherent in the initial act of installing the machine as a metaphor in architecture. The process of installing the machine as a metaphor in architecture found another expression in the fact that buildings came to be increasingly designed not only to resemble machines in their operations but their shapes were also determined by the operational capacities of the machine, that is, by what the highly mechanized construction processes could produce most efficiently. The discussion of the whole problem of technology, that is, of the transformation of city and world through the introduction of machines, has been strangely led astray by an all-too-exclusive concentration upon the service or disservice that machines render to humans. This discussion is based on an assumption that the primary function of all tools and implements of humankind is to extend the efficiency of human limbs and to make human labor less painful. The instrumentality is understood exclusively in this anthropocentric sense. "But the instrumentality of tools and implements," as Hannah Arendt has pointed out,

> is much more closely related to the object it is designed to produce and their sheer "human value" is restricted to the use the *animal laborans* make of them. In other words, *homo faber*, the toolmaker, invented tools and implements in order to erect a world, not—at least not primarily—to help the human life process. The question therefore is not so much whether we are the masters or the slaves of our machines, but whether machines still serve the world and its things, or if, on the contrary, they and the automatic motion of their processes have begun to rule and even destroy world and things.[5]

To be sure, the myth of the optimum efficiency of the human hand guided by the human brain was shattered soon enough by the continuous process of automation. John Diebold, for example, told us in 1952 that "the greatest pitfall to avoid is the assumption that the design aim is reproduction of the hand movement of the operator or laborer."[6] But more important was the fact that the continuous automation process had also done away with the assumption that the things of the human-made world around us should depend upon human design and be built in accordance with human standards of utility, beauty and firmness. The nineteenth century had already seen the inherent equality of utility, beauty and firmness, in the original Vitruvian triad, shifted to a new equation whereby beauty was seen as a function of utility and firmness. It was only necessary now to replace the dual standards of utility and firmness with a singular standard of process. In place of utility, beauty and firmness, which are standards of the world, we have come to design products and buildings that still fulfill certain basic functions, the functions of the human animal's life process, and are firm enough to stand, but whose designs will be primarily determined by, and analogous to, the operation of the machine. Hence Le Corbusier's declaration, "a house is a machine for living in."[7]

The effort to place process or change at the center of architectural theory has led to the distinct formal attitudes of our time. The increasing preoccupation with change and growth in the mid-twentieth century has produced an aesthetics of process. This sought to project an image of the changing world by distinguishing between various elements of the building as those which are relatively constant or stable and those which are likely to undergo programmatic or formal change. At best this produced, as in the case of the Berlin Free University, an order expressing the dynamics of life. The project was conceived as a deeply interconnected three-dimensional city with internal streets, squares, courtyards and multiple walkways. At best the structure of the whole organization allowed the articulation of several spatial and constructive elements to respond to different demands of use and provided an incredible variety of ambiences within a controlled modular system. At worst it spawned a whole series of "plug-in" architectures, either of the Japanese "metabolist" variety (Figure 1.6) or of the British "Archigram," reducing architecture to a game, like Lego blocks, whereby elements of a building are conceived of as not only potentially changeable; in actuality their replacement when they become outdated has already been planned for; a kind of planned obsolescence. The fact that some of the images produced by the "Archigram" group resembled parts of human anatomy or that the Japanese called themselves the "metabolists" indicated the biological basis of their thinking. It also meant, in retrospect, that the machine as a metaphor in architecture was, in a subtle way, being replaced by something far closer to human anatomy. The biological under-pinning of those movements of the 1960s has survived and found expression in the more recent "post-modern" discipline of formal composition, which accepts the increasing fragmentation of life as given and seeks to present an image of it through a composition of equally fragmented architectural forms extracted from our academic dictionary and plugged in, as it were, to a new relationship.

The modern consciousness has been shaped, more than anything else, by the increasing rate of change. No one knows this better than those of us who live in or around New York City in this first quarter of the twenty-first century. Rushed by the cumulative momentum of science and technology, the tension, vibration and the pace of change are incalculably greater today than they were at the turn of the last century. Nothing defines our age more than the furious and relentless increase in the rate of this change. Science makes, dissolves, rebuilds and extends our environment every day.

This has meant, above all, that life is perceived as motion and not as order; that the universe is seen not as complete but as in a process of creation. The aesthetic ideal of the West from the ancient Greeks through the nineteenth cen-tury has been to see life steadily and see it whole. That possibility was one of the first casualties of the increasing velocity of history. Seeing life at once steadily and whole was plausible enough when the artist and their environment had a stable relationship over time. Gertrude Stein described the twentieth century well as "a time when everything cracks, where everything is destroyed, every-thing isolates itself."[8]

The modern consciousness, compelled by changes in the external environment to a vivid awareness of time, mutability, novelty, chance and inter-connection, saw the universe as open, indeterminate and interrelated with time. The search for techniques expressive of the fragmentation wrought by the increasing acceleration of life characterizes much of modern architecture as it does much of modern painting, music, sculpture and literature. It is recalled by such words as "apartness," "discordance," "incongruity" and "irresolution." In other words, to present life and reality as it is.

The fragmentation was inherent in the contradictions built into the initial assumption. To design objects for the operational capacities, or limitations, of the machine instead of designing machines for the production of certain objects which would constitute the human-made world, and to install process as a source of validity for the formal qualities of a work of architecture, would indeed be the exact reversal of the means–end category, if this category still made any sense. But more disturbing than the loss of the means–end category is the fact that the reciprocity and inter-dependence between nature and culture, between the world of human-made things and things as nature provides them is fast disappearing. It is in a way a reversal of the *from nature to culture* phenomenon for which the means–end category is a precondition.

Instruments, tools and machines belong to the activity of producing things which surround us and which transcend and outlive the actual process of producing. Process itself has no presence. While it is in the nature of being to appear and disclose itself, it is in the nature of process to remain invisible, "to be something whose existence can only be inferred from the presence of certain phenomena."[9] Thus, without the existence of the means–end category, it is obvious that the crucial distinction between nature (the repository of all processes including the life process) and culture (the repository of all human-made things) would itself disappear. When Louis Kahn said that "man is born of nature but is not nature," he was referring to the reciprocity between humans and nature, and the need to sustain this distinction between the world of humans and the world of nature. As Hannah Arendt said in 1958:

> without taking things out of nature's hand and consuming them, and without defending himself against the natural processes of growth and decay, the *animal labourans* could never survive. But, at the same time, being at home in the midst of things whose durability makes them fit for use and for erecting a world whose very permanence stands in direct contrast to natural life, this life would never be human.[10]

This gradual coming together of nature and culture has taken many forms. Since the discovery of processes by the natural and social sciences has coincided with the discovery of introspection in philosophy, it is only natural that the biological process within ourselves should eventually become the very model of the new concept. The crudest expression of this is the modern superstition that "money begets money" or probably the sharpest political insight that "power generates power." There are many other such expressions which owe their plausibility to the underlying metaphors of the natural fertility of life, a phenomenon not to be found in the world of human-made things, which requires the intervention of human hand to make anything.

Only under one condition can the biological process be objectified, made visible, and that is by devaluing or debasing the human-made things of the world, including tools, instruments and machines, from their position of things that make up this world to commodities of consumption. "Only by being a part of the never-ending natural process of man's metabolism with nature, by acquiring an exchange value in the cycle of consumption and regeneration, can the objective world symbolize process."[11] Claus Oldenberg's proposal to erect a giant banana as a monument in the middle of Times Square is not only a comment on the values of a society which predetermines what is trivia and what is profound, but also draws our attention to the increasing trivialization of that which is profound. The increasing subjectivization of the objective world of things, that is the need to possess, consume, handle and constantly renew our gadgets, instruments, cars, buildings and so on has elevated the element of novelty to the level of profound. This and the so-called consumer economy have created a second nature of humans which ties them biologically and aggressively to the commodity form. It is biological in the sense in which inclinations, behavior patterns and aspirations become vital needs which, if not satisfied, would cause dysfunction of the organism. If biological needs are defined as those which must be satisfied and for which no adequate substitute can be provided, certain cultural needs can "sink down" into the biology of humans. We could then speak, for example, of some aesthetic needs as having taken root in the organic structure of humans, in their *nature* or rather *second nature*.

This amounts to a fundamental devaluation, or debasement, of the objective world around us and, by implication, of humans themselves. The human-made world of things, buildings and cities which constituted the public realm by its relative permanence can no more guarantee this permanence if it is seen as potentially consumable. Cities, buildings and things which are the result of humans' efforts to build a world which distinguishes them from nature are meant to outlast their authors and in this relative permanence lies the objective qualities of the public realm without which people cannot be human. To deprive the architecture of this world the capacity to carry any public ideas, that is, to deprive it of its qualities as a discourse, is to deprive humans of the very public realm in which cultures are built from the raw materials of nature. This discursive quality had already suffered a severe blow in the early nineteenth century when, as a result of the inspiration of the machine, form was seen as valid only to the extent that it contributed positively to the operations within the building: the building as a use object, a *clockwork*. But even as use objects buildings do constitute the objective world, the world that can unmistakably proclaim the presence of humans on this earth. But the use of this imagery of the machine in architecture, as we have seen, was subtly and gradually replaced by a far more biological imagery. And the very possibilities opened up by the machine itself have something to do with this.

Humans have always dreamed of freeing themselves from nature. This has often been misinterpreted in terms of an adversarial relationship between humans and nature. The desire was always to express, through cultural constructions, a reciprocity with nature, which requires a degree of independence from nature rather than superiority over it. It was felt that the emancipation of humans from the laboring process of producing their food from nature, consuming it and excreting the remains back into nature, which tied them metabolically with the natural cycle of creation, growth and decay, would free humans from nature. The abundance of consumable objects and commodities achieved partly through the productivity of machines and partly through violence over nature, seemed to realize the age-old dream of this emancipation.

Figure 2.2
**Painting
showing the
interior of the
Crystal Palace,
Hyde Park,
London, UK,
1851.**

But the commodity character of an object is far more integrally tied up with the exchange value of an object in the marketplace of humans than with the use-value, its instrumentality. With the various world exhibitions around in the nineteenth century (Figure 2.2), the enthronement of the consumable, exchangeable commodity as a new deity, in place of the useful machine, was complete. The exhibitions quickly became the places of pilgrimage to the fetish commodity, and were festivals of emancipation for the working class.

As Walter Benjamin has noted, "Fashion prescribed the ritual by which the fetish commodity wished to be worshipped. Fetishism, which succumbs to the sex appeal of the inorganic, is its vital nerve; and the cult of the commodity recruits this to its service."[12] The fantasies of the advertisement transmitted this commodity character onto the world of objects.

But we must ask if the dream of emancipation has been realized by relying upon the commodity character of human products. The loaf of bread that humans produced out of the elements of nature did not free them from nature because it was consumed as soon as it was produced and thus did not constitute the objective world. But the tools and instruments that helped humans in producing the bread did outlive the consumption of bread and began to erect and constitute a world which nature itself could never have produced without the help of humans. Still neither the loaf of bread, which is also a product of humans, nor the tools and instrument constituted a public realm in the sense that neither of them carried, in their reification, recognition of the presence of another human being. Humans can go on making bread and can even have instruments to help them in this endeavor, but will still remain tied to nature so long as this activity is confined to the satisfaction of their biological needs. It is only when the things humans make transcend their instrumentality and derive their validity instead from moral and ethical considerations that humans can truly be free from nature without being antagonistic towards nature. Thus to rely upon the abundance of consumable objects and things to realize humankind's dream of freedom leads not to freedom but only an illusion of freedom. The irony of the situation is that humankind's dream of emancipation through the abundance of commodities can be realized only by turning the human-built world, which distinguished humans from nature, into a commodity of consumption, like a loaf of bread, and in the process merging humans with nature more than ever before. This dream can have a charm of its own so long as it is a dream, but it turns into a fool's paradise as soon as it is realized.

It is obvious that a significant detour in the history of architecture occurred when it was felt that architecture must be accountable to the strictly rational qualities of mind. This, coupled with an almost narcissistic concern with the comfort of the human body and the pleasures of the senses, displaced the objective of architecture from that of building *good* buildings to *useful* buildings to merely *beautiful* buildings. Whereas *good* implies both aesthetic and ethical dimensions, merely *beautiful* is, strictly speaking, apolitical and extra moral. It is interesting to remember here the comment of Walter Benjamin quoted earlier about Fourier's Phalanstery, which he said "has to lead men back into relations in which morality would become superfluous." But morality resides in the public realm. "Having a moral end in view," says Romaldo Giurgola "implies having a public end in view, both imply a rededication among architects to their proper role in society."[13] But such rededication is by no means a matter of course. Against it stands the conviction of those who would judge architecture in terms of its usefulness to supposedly higher ends to make the world more "useful" and more "beautiful," or to make life easier and longer. They would probably incline to denounce any consideration of architecture as a work of art, as idleness or vagueness. But all the great architecture of the past, including that of the past two centuries, came to be as a result of a desire to make good architecture first and foremost. They are the places where "aesthetics and ethics were inextricably joined in the same practical system which provided the basis both for the construction of buildings and the creation of works of art."[14] This quality comes about when an intense identification with the essence of the materials of nature is achieved, this identification and recognition of the fact that the human sense of reality demands initiatives which are morally and ethically justifiable. It is an initiative from which no human being can refrain and still be human. It is this initiative which is always present in a work of art.

When these images are fragmented and the pieces are inserted, like quoted texts, in a new architectural object, what they convey is not so much the image of a fragmented, high-speed life but an image of a society which has, somehow, lost any memory of a beginning. These partial images borrow only the formal qualities of their prototypes and exclude any question of why they were made the way they were in the beginning. In other words they take a neutral, extra moral, non-ideological position and justify it by interpreting the role of architecture as that of merely reflecting, indiscriminately like a mirror, the complexities and meanings of a supposedly fragmented and pluralistic culture. But dissociated from the circumstances of their beginning these architectural virtual images focus exclusively upon the object per se; that is, aesthetics without ethical or moral dimension. Such aestheticism is a fool's paradise which dissipates the moment it is realized.

Notes

1   Paul Ricoeur, *History and Truth* (Evanston: Northwestern University Press, 1965), 271.

2   Walter Benjamin, "Paris: Capital of the Nineteenth Century," *Perspecta*, 12 (1969), 163–172.

3   Thomas Carlyle, *The French Revolution: A History* (London: Chapman & Hall, 1896), 53.

4   Lord William Kelvin, "Electrical Units of Measurement." In *Popular Lectures and Addresses (1891–1894)*, vol.1, quoted at http://zapatopi.net/kelvin/quotes/html.

5   Hannah Arendt, *The Human Condition* (Chicago: University of Chicago Press, 1958), 151.

6   John T. Diebold, *Automation: The Advent of the Automatic Factory* (Princeton: Van Nostrand, 1952), 67.

7   Le Corbusier, *Towards a New Architecture* (New York: Dover Publications, 1986), 4.

8   Gertrude Stein, *Picasso* (London: B.T. Batsford, 1939), 49–50. Quoted in Ronald E. Martin, *American Literature and the Destruction of Knowledge* (Durham, NC: Duke University Press, 1991), 180.

9   Hannah Arendt, op. cit., 296–297.

10 Ibid.,135.

11 Ibid.

12 Water Benjamin, op. cit.

13 Romando Giurgola, "Notes on Architecture and Morality," *Precis*, 2 (1980), 51–52.

14 Ibid.

Chapter 3

Interrogative Scholarship

Theorizing the Agenda for Post-Rational Architecture

Exploring the theoretical postulates of modernism in architecture, we realize that the movement was ideologically anchored to the ideas inherent in the predominant "thought-world" of Western civilization, whose roots ran all the way down to ancient Greece. Recent scholarship in the West and elsewhere is beginning to reveal that since ancient times not only did other thought-worlds exist, such as the Persian and Indian, but also that these were often entangled in a "web in which an element in one culture often leads to elements in others."[1] This story of diffusion seems to have lasted until the Enlightenment in Europe. The relative isolation of European scholars from distant lands and cultures immediately preceding the colonial period was the reason for their ignorance of these thought-worlds and provided fertile soil for colonial scholars to construct what Edward Said later termed "Orientalism," in which the West used Asia as the Other to construct its self-identity. In this intellectual milieu, this binary of the West and the Rest is still sub-consciously affecting architectural scholarship.

Architectural scholarship, especially in India, has not been able to fully resolve this binary of India and the West. It has been more than 60 years since India attained political independence from its colonial European rulers. But even before the European hold over the Indian mind during the last three centuries began, there have been a number of other inputs, such as Persian, Jewish and Islamic, and not all of these have had such detrimental consequences as the European. The English Education Act of 1835, prompted by Lord Macaulay's *Minute upon Indian Education*, radically shifted the axis of intellectual endeavors in India from which we have not yet recovered. Still, the imposition of the English language or the alien structures of learning by themselves are not as detrimental as the underlying problem of philosophical relativism that has been at play throughout the colonial occupation of our minds. As Professor Jitendranath Mohanty has succinctly observed, this relativism tells us that,

> the oriental, the Indian or the Chinese, or for that matter, any other "radically different" community does not do "philosophy" *in that sense* in which the idea of philosophy was originally instituted by the Greeks. "Philosophy", along with its implied concept of rationality, is typically western. If the Hindus or the Buddhists did something they today call philosophy, that is not philosophy in the standard western sense; their concept of rationality

is radically different from the western. What they call "their" "logic" is not "ours", these "logics" differ not as Aristotelian from that of the *Principia Mathematica*, but so radically that the same word "logic" can only be used at the risk of equivocation. It is not uncommon to say that the Orientals did not *think*, that they did not raise their intuitions to the level of "concepts", that their philosophies are in fact religions (and that their religions are intuitive, aesthetic, not conceptual), and so on and so forth.[2]

Epistemologically, this assumes that the West can have access to the oriental thought-worlds only by transforming them into Western constructs and interpreting them in the West's own terms. But the moment you raise such a possibility, you realize that it leads to the denial of the very binary you began with and to the assumption that there is only one system with its own language and all others are translatable into it. Such an assumption already exists. Paul Ricoeur, writing about the possibility of a syncretic universal civilization in 1965, said "science does not foster this power of unifying mankind because it is Greek or European but because it is a human dimension. It manifests a sort of *de jure* unity which controls all the other features of civilization."[3] In other words, science, with its implied rationality, is a universal attribute and any other claim of being scientific will have to measure up to that level of rationality. Many thinkers, especially philosophers, both Indian and Western, have been able to overcome this dilemma and have, over the past century, produced insightful understanding of the overlapping contents of both thought systems while preserving the otherness of the other. But in other areas and forms of knowledge—and here I must limit myself to scholarship in architecture—this is not the case.

This prevents Indian architecture and scholarly writings from effectively connecting with intellectual development in the rest of the world. This situation manifests at two levels. First, Indian architects who also explore ideas (and there are some brilliant scholars writing insightful essays) almost always limit their thematic concerns to those within the Indian civilizational boundary and its history and traditions. They hardly ever engage with ideas emerging from the rest of the world. At best, their explorations are rooted in the Indian soil and are informed by immense knowledge and wisdom developed over the centuries by great Indian thinkers. They refer to the plurality of Indian life, art, literature, philosophy and belief systems to draw inferences for the present. However, while it is important and necessary to look critically at architectural production in India, to explain the past and to guide the present, these efforts remain mostly self-referential and miss the opportunity to *interrogate* the two streams of thought from the relative perspectives of each other.

Second, Western observers who have written about contemporary Indian architecture have mostly seen it as appropriate and relevant only within the social, cultural and environmental conditions of India without realizing or acknowledging its global value. No doubt such efforts are well intentioned but, on closer scrutiny one realizes that they have failed to notice that contemporary Indian architects such as B.V. Doshi, Charles Correa, Achyut Kanvinde, Habib Rahman and others, not unlike Geoffrey Bawa of Sri Lanka and Hassan Fathy of Egypt, have been engaged not only in evolving an architectural language rooted in their cultural soil but also in articulating an alternative idea of modernity—'universal modernity' to coin a term—transcending its Eurocentric techno-rational definition. This universal modernity involves embracing scientific rigor and rationality while being sensitive to the specificity of the architect's respective culture and location, which also values non-rationality. This has not been noticed or commented upon by Western observers. One would like to believe that this may be due to Western scholars' inability to fathom the complexity and plurality of India and its various thought systems, which has undoubtedly informed its architecture. On the other hand, it may also amount to an unwillingness on the part of Western observers to confront the fact that the identity of modern architecture, as constructed to align it with modern science and industry, has been inadequate and needs to be enlarged to encompass other values. It has been clear for some time now that inherent contradictions of theoretical postulates have informed modern architecture and its built productions. The idea of modernity (as opposed to modernism), which began in Europe in the sixteenth century, was premised on the desire to overcome the tyranny of religion and tradition and provide a rational basis for day-to-day life. Modernity is an idea which connotes a certain way of life, a way of thinking and doing. This cultural modernity was aimed at the division of substantive reason expressed in religion and metaphysics into three autonomous spheres: science, morality and art. It is evident that this modernist movement was an all-encompassing paradigm shift involving a fundamental change in worldview which began in Europe but is now spreading fast to other parts of the world in various degrees. This is an ongoing project that is still being pursued by many societies around the world and which must continue.

Modernism, on the other hand, is an ism, a political ideology specifying a plan of action to usher in modernity. It ended up installing reason as the legitimising force for all human endeavors. *Modernism*, so narrowly defined, has not lived up to its promise to represent a cultural *modernity* premised on an all-encompassing knowledge revolution. Other non-Western societies have developed different ways of seeing and making the environment which are equally valid and offer the critical foil, the "other" by which to unravel the taken-for-granted assumptions of the dominant Western view of the world, and works done outside Europe have the potential to offer a course correction. But this requires engagement at the much deeper level of the ideologies that invariably inform architectural choices. *Critical Regionalism*[4] has recently been advanced as an alternative approach to both modernism as well as post-modernism. It stems from a position, correct I believe, that both later approaches are problematic. However, the extent to which it still seeks a singular, syncretic, universal architectural theory, I find less convincing. Precluding any authentic dialog between thought-worlds, it proposes an architectural unity founded on reason and technology, which are assumed to have no local domain, while accepting the plurality of local sensibilities to express the specificity of the place. That the absence of placeness has been one of the major infirmities of modernism is true, but geography has less to do with this than humans' conceptions about themselves and the relative values assigned to the human temporal and causal order and the logical one. Above all, these values are concerned with what constitutes reality, truth and beauty.

Is there a way to overcome this either/or situation? Can there be a universal acceptance that there are other modes of thinking, others in a genuine sense, which may be accessible to us? I believe there can be only if we accept three conditions. One, all of us, Indian and Western, have to transcend our own thought-worlds. Although each of us and each culture has our or its own "world" it is possible to reflect on one's own world objectively. We can thus transcend our own world-boundedness and locate ourselves within the other mode of thinking. Two, we must accept that each of these "worlds," howsoever different they may be from each other, have overlapping contents. And three, it is here in these overlapping contents where similarities and differences are starkly perceptible, that a potentiality of diffusion may exist through this reflective process of trying to make sense of each other.

Theorizing has always been an adjunct activity of architectural practice. Throughout history and in all civilizations, architects have been engaged in the construction of edifices and also in exploring ideas about architecture. The latter may range from simple codification of the artisanal practices, through explanations and interpretation, to advocacy of a particular way of doing architecture. In most cases, though, the earliest writings are almost always in the form of codification of the prevailing best practices. The West has an almost unbroken tradition of architectural scholarship—if we ignore the 1,400-year gap between Vitruvius and Alberti, the two first scholar/architects to shape and set the agenda for much of the architecture in the Renaissance and up to the eighteenth century. Since then, however, there has been a proliferation of scholarship in the West that continues unabated today. This offers us an excellent opportunity to excavate possible thought-worlds that may lie beneath the surface of apparent interests.

Elsewhere, I have referred to this as the "emergence of academic architecture,"[5] an architecture of ideas that parallels and informs the production of built forms, which must now be reflected upon at a theoretical level. Its co-emergence with the strong grip the rationalist/determinist thought-world had acquired over European society must be interrogated to understand modernist thought and discourse in architecture over the last two centuries. The reason being that the aesthetic language produced by this discourse has in turn produced a perceptible alienation between society and its built environment. This can be directly attributed to the emergence and development of academic tradition in architecture. The scholarship brought to bear on this enterprise by Fra Carlo Lodoli and Marc-Antoine Laugier in the eighteenth century, Julien Guadet and Auguste Choisy in the nineteenth century, and finally Sigfried Giedion, J.M. Richards, and Henry-Russell Hitchcock and Philip Johnson in the twentieth century was different from the earlier attempts at codification by Vitruvius, Palladio or Alberti. While Classical and Renaissance scholars sought to sublimate their own experience, as well as historical evidence, into codification as a guide to practice, later writers attempted to *interpret* historical data and construct a coherent narrative to align architecture with the prevailing Rationalism.

For example, while analyzing Mies van der Rohe's Barcelona pavilion and the Tugendhat house in Brno, Sigfried Giedion eloquently describes the "new space conception" and its "flowing interpenetration of space." But this analysis ends with a rather off-handed remark about the perceptual qualities of the same space: "Even so, one does not get away from the feeling of being exposed to an aquarium-like existence."[6] This obviously betrays a bias in favor of the new space conception. The other qualities of the space are only grudgingly acknowledged. Thus history, far from being a factual representation of the past, is a human-made cultural construct for the very process of selection involves *foregrounding* of a certain part of the past which then gets etched in our collective consciousness as truth. On the other hand, as Reyner Banham has noted, the professional body,

> while repudiating the "false standards of academies," accepted many academic ideas without knowing where they had come from. Thus Gropius in 1923, having criticized the academies for not nurturing aesthetic science, goes on in the succeeding paragraphs to make use of a number of aesthetic concepts that resemble those of French academic origin.[7]

The above makes it clear that scholarship had a far greater role to play in the development of the direction architecture took in the twentieth century and by interrogating it, as we have done above, we uncover the fact that the exclusivity accorded to *reason*, among all human faculties, is the darker side of the Enlightenment: "an unreasonable reason has brought man to a situation where he begins to be alienated from his production and from the natural world."[8] At the height of the Enlightenment, Descartes' method was rooted in verification: the only path to truth, and thus knowledge, was through axioms derived from observation. Descartes' insistence that the sure and indubitable should form the basis of reasoning had an obvious impact on the prevailing views of logic and discourse. But an alternative view existed, that of Giambattista Vico (1668–1744). Vico inaugurated a school of thought which later came to be known as Phenomenology, which argued against the primacy accorded to reason at the expense of other human faculties, such as intuition and perception, and for the compatibility between the human temporal and causal order and the logical one. But the Cartesian/Kantian view got foregrounded as Vico remained mostly in the academic libraries, until his resurrection in the twentieth century.

Confronted with this rationalist-determinist and logico-scientific worldview of much of the modern thinking, we are left wondering why, and how, rationality, a universal attribute of humankind, came to be limited to the Western thought-world. This would amount to limiting the notion of rationality as "Western rationality," a non-universal attribute, and in the process destroying the very essence of the idea of "rationality" as the universal attribute of humankind. As J.N. Mohanty has pointed out, philosophy, as the purest form of rational inquiry, must be seen as being capable of containing differentiation and diversity. This diversity is manifested in the simultaneous existence of the Indian philosophical tradition known as *darsana* as well as the Greek *philosophia*.[9]

At its core, rationality deals with truth, the source of knowledge of truth and the method for arriving at, and validating, truth. Of course, Indian thinkers, ancient and modern, have expended considerable energy on this question, but if you ask any of them what the concept of rationality is in Indian thought, you are unlikely to get an answer for Indian thought on this matter moves along a different path. As Arindam Chakrabarti has noted:

> Of the four features of Indian thought that could be pointed out as reasons for skepticism about the very idea of an Indian conception of Rationality the first that draws our attention is the alleged practical or goal-oriented character of Indian philosophy. Not only are pleasure (*kama*), power/wealth (*artha*), piety/righteousness (*dharma*), and final liberation from suffering (*moksa*) distinguished as the four—and only four—alternative and actually pursued goals of life, but even branches of knowledge or subjects of study are divided accordingly. Thus we have *kamasastra, arthasastra, dharmasastra*, and a specially prestigious *moksasastra* dealing with these four goals respectively. Philosophy is often identified with the last of these, so that there remains no room for the pure theories of logic, mathematics, knowledge, reality, or morality, undertaken simply for the sake of intellectual satisfaction.[10]

One way in which we understand "rationality" is as a differentiating feature distinguishing human beings from other animals. Indian thinkers have also addressed this issue but have arrived at a startlingly different conclusion. For example, *Mahabharata* contains several verses explaining that humans are great because they have a pair of hands with ten pliable digits with which they can take out thorns, and make tools, shelters and clothing. Thus not so much as *homo sapiens* but as *homo faber* do humans rule over other creatures.

Thus, to determine a concept of rationality for a culture, we need to consider first what makes a belief, for that culture, acceptable as truth; second, what makes an action appropriate, normatively right and authentic; and, finally, what makes a work of art beautiful. According to Mohanty, consciousness (*cit*) is the ultimate ground of all evidence (*siddhi*). However, this consciousness does not distinguish between truth and falsity; it is neutral and establishes both. In order to establish truth, "the Indian philosophers, in different ways, take recourse to a theory of '*pramana*' meaning *both* the specific *cause* of true cognition and also the means of validating or justifying cognitive claims."[11]

While *pramana* (veridical cognition) as a source of knowledge is accepted by all sub-schools of Indian philosophy, there are differences regarding its sources. In all we come across the following six, of which the first two are common to all schools of thought.

1. *Pratyaksha* (perception), the knowledge gained by means of the senses;
2. *Anumāna* (inference), the knowledge gained by means of inference or reference;
3. *Śabda* (verbal testimony), the knowledge gained by verbal testimony of teachers or scriptures;
4. *Upamāna* (comparison), the knowledge gained by means of analogy;

5. *Arthāpatti* (postulation), something taken as self-evident or assumed without proof as a basis for reasoning; and

6. *Anupalabdi* (non-cognition), non-apprehension and scepticism in the face of non-apprehension.

It is interesting to note that, in this matter of how to arrive at truth, plurality of beliefs was allowed to persist without it being resolved into a singular conception. It is a characteristic of the Indian thought system that a bewildering range of conflicting narratives often existed and each of these held special significance for the school(s) of thought that subscribed to it. However, according to the twelfth-century logician Gangesa Upadhyaya, *pratyaksha* is the first in the cognitive hierarchy and is not caused by any other cognition.[12] Nevertheless, rationality was not totally absent from Indian thought: it was exercised, together with perception, in the forms of inference, comparison, postulation and scepticism. In fact, *nyaya*, one of the schools of thought, implies judgment about reality arrived at by reasoned inquiry. Thus the theory of *pramana* does not distinguish but "incorporates in its body the causal and the logical orders in one. This limits the ideality of the logical and the contingency of the causal—as it must, if the two orders are to coincide."[13] This locates the theory of *pramana* in the ontological realm of the objective world.

It is the third form of *pramana, sabda* (word) that is the most intriguing and least convincing as seen from the shores of the Western thought-world. It has a profound implication on our present concern about architectural scholarship. It proposes that there is a form of cognition that is entirely word-generated (*sabda-janya*) and is founded on the belief that the Vedic language itself is a source of knowledge about whatever lies beyond the range of sensory perception. It implies the validity of knowledge of moral rules, spiritual goals and practical action (including that of making the world, the action of *homo faber*), which are derived from reading, interpreting and understanding the spiritual texts. Here, I allude to the present attempts, by a section of architectural scholars, to revive *Vaastu Shastra*, the ancient scriptural wisdom on architecture. But *sabda* involves not only reading the works, but also listening to the spoken utterances of those authors who are considered intellectually and morally superior, that is, to authority. This authority is supposed to be the scriptures and those who claim to speak for the scriptures. This not only negates any role played by either perception or inference but also implies that the theory of *pramana* has a built-in contradiction. As Mohanty has pointed out, "If *sabda* is a *pramana* . . ., then one cannot challenge word-generated cognition as uncritical; that would amount to imposing a critical norm that is not in consonance with those of the theory itself."[14]

That the word, written or spoken, is a source of knowledge is a truism; otherwise, it will be pointless for me to write these words or speak to my students in a seminar. But implied here is the fact that if my words raise questions, there are always other words that might challenge or correct me. *Sabda* corrects *sabda*. Thus the text always leaves room for interpretive differences and new possibilities for interpretation. It is when this door to interpretive corrections are closed that the text becomes dogma. My guess is that *sabda* may be a late insertion during the medieval period of the *Puranas* coinciding with the rise of the *bhakti* (devotion) movement. During this period a proliferation of texts, covering all walks of life, occurred. Of particular interest to us is the body of texts which we know today under the umbrella term of *Vaastu Shastra*. *Vaastu Shastra*, as a compilation of ancient wisdom on architecture, has existed as part of our Vedic and Upanishadic heritage for centuries. This has been passed on through generations via collective memories, "*smruti*" (remembered) and "*shruti*"[15] (heard). This wisdom was always receptive to new interpretation as is evident from the many open and stimulating public debates recorded in history between scholars, often lasting for several days. And of course, the fact that more than half a dozen schools of thought co-existed without agreeing on everything suggests the non-doctrinaire nature of Vedic thought. It was during the late *Puranic* period (500–1500 CE) that *Vaastu Shastra* came to be written down in simpler language to make it accessible to common people, and it gradually acquired the aura of inviolable scripture. During the last few decades it has captured the interest of many as something that may offer solutions to our problems, even for modern problems that were not envisaged by our ancestors, and for that reason needs to be revived. However, in its present form it is mostly seen as a series of prescriptions and proscriptions, supposedly laid down by the scriptures, for constructing our earthly habitat. Opinions vary about the beneficial, or otherwise, effects of these practices. But these developments do generate a suspicion that the very presence of the theory of word-generated cognition might undermine the otherwise critical nature of the theory of *pramana*.

However, if the practice of architecture involves not only the knowledge of the empirical facts of the methods and techniques of construction, which are perceptible and thus inferable by ordinary means, but also our knowledge of the aesthetic, moral and ethical rules and spiritual goals, then *sabda* has a pretty good reason to be a *pramana*. In the contemporary context I interpret *sabda* to mean more critical scholarship more subject to interpretation than inviolable scriptures. After all, the interpretation of linguistic discourse has always been built into the Indian philosophical traditions. The fact that there existed several schools of thought, such as *Nyaya*, *Sankhya* or *Vedanta*, whose list of *pramanas* and also their basic understanding of *pramanas* differed from each other, all of which defended their respective positions in open public debates with equal convictions, points to a healthy acceptance of interpretation during the pre-*puranic* age of the Upanishads. Architecture deals with two parallel streams of knowledge; the empirical facts of technology and the materiality of buildings, which are inferred (grasped through knowing and verifiable) and the moral, ethical, spiritual and aesthetic aspects, which are sensed (grasped through the intuitive understanding of the situation at hand). Architecture must embrace both these streams of knowledge. As for the moral, ethical, spiritual and aesthetic aspects, the rules for determining what one ought or ought not to do may be determined by reading, listening to and interpreting linguistic discourse. However, to obey uncritically a competent speaker or text, to do or not to do what it says, would be to infer that the words so uttered or written embody those moral or ethical rules as if they were cast in stone. Mohanty makes the point that we learn the rules only from hearing/reading and interpreting verbal instructions . . . if an accepted set of moral rules is given up, it is given up by imbibing another set of moral rules on the basis of another set of verbal instructions.[16]

In other words, new scholarship may correct or modify the old scholarship.

Unfortunately, scholarship is a rare attribute among contemporary Indian architects: it is actually looked down upon. This has produced much of our characterless urban landscape. Both Western knowledge and ancient Indian traditions have given us discursive reasoning, albeit from varied perspectives. But when it comes to architecture we display either structural and functional determinism or uncritical adherence to past practices without understanding their true meanings. Rejecting rationalism as a dogma should not amount to rejecting the exercise of reasoning. It is here that one sees a possible overlap between the two thought-worlds of India and the West. Phenomenology, as a philosophical movement, inaugurated by Edmund Husserl in Europe, and simultaneously by K.C. Bhattacharyya in India in the early twentieth century, exhibits a remarkable coincidence with the theory of *pramana*. Both these schools of philosophy are primarily concerned with the systematic reflection on and study of the structures of consciousness and the phenomena that appear in acts of consciousness (*noema* in Greek and *cit* in Sanskrit). Phenomenology offers architecture a possible avenue for theorizing future direction in which both reason and experience will co-exist.

The existential and ontological issues which such a confluence throws up are particularly significant for architecture, which ultimately rests with the lived experience of humans in their phenomenal environment. Modernity is still an ongoing and incomplete project and its architecture will be post-rational architecture wherein reason will be moderated by the phenomenological and experiential qualities so as, to restate what Mohanty has said, to limit "the ideality of the logical and the contingency of the causal."

Notes

1   Thomas McEvilly, *The Shape of Ancient Thought* (New York: Allworth Press, 2002), 1.

2   Jitendra Nath Mohanty, "The Concept of Rationality." In *Phenomenology and Indian Philosophy*, ed. Debi Prasad Chattopadhyaya, Lester E. Embree and Jitendra Nath Mohanty (Albany: SUNY Press, 1992), 9.

3   Paul Ricoeur, *History and Truth* (Evanston: Northwestern University Press, 1965), 272.

4   Liane Lefaivre and Alexander Tzonis, *Critical Regionalism, Architecture and Identity in a Globalized World* (Munich, Berlin, London and New York: Prestel, 2003), and Kenneth Frampton, "Towards a Critical Regionalism: Six Points for an Architecture of Resistance." In *The Anti-Aesthetic: Essays on Postmodern Culture*, ed. Hal Foster (Seattle: Bay Press, 1983), 21.

5   Jaimini Mehta, *Rethinking Modernity: Towards Post-Rational Architecture* (New Delhi: Niyogi Books, 2011), 11–20.

6   Sigfried Giedion, *Space, Time and Architecture* (Cambridge, MA: Harvard University Press, 1962), 545.

7   Reyner Banham, *Theory and Design in the First Machine Age* (New York: Praeger, 1972), 15.

8 Kenneth Frampton, *Modern Architecture: A Critical History* (New York: Oxford University Press, 1980), 9.

9 Jitendra Nath Mohanty, *Reason and Tradition in Indian Thought* (Oxford: Clarendon Press, 2002), 7, 8.

10 Arindam Chakrabarti, "Rationality in Indian Philosophy." In *A Companion to World Philosophies*, ed. E. Deutsch and R. Bontekoe (Oxford, 1991), 259–278.

11 Jitendra Nath Mohanty, "The Concept of Rationality," 10.

12 Sibajiban Bhattacharyya, *Gangesa's Theory of Indeterminate Perception* (New Delhi, Indian Council of Philosophical Research, 1993).

13 Jitendra Nath Mohanty, ibid., 13.

14 Ibid., 16.

15 "*Shruti*," literally meaning "heard," is often interpreted to mean authorless text or (divine) revelation. However, it may also mean intuitive realization of eternal ideas or truth by sensitive minds, which are then passed on to later generations in textual form.

16 Jitendra Nath Mohanty, ibid., 16.

Chapter 4

Contingent Criticality

The two years from 1968 to 1970 were watershed years for architectural education in the West. The eruption first at the École des Beaux-Arts in Paris followed by those at Harvard and Columbia universities found the students of architecture in the vanguard. As Giancarlo De Carlo has analyzed, the students

> began to realize it was a question not only of organizational structures and teaching methods, but rather of the purpose of their preparation; in broader terms, of their social destination. The objective of their struggle therefore could no longer be simply to substitute new symbols for old symbols and new men for old men. Instead it was a question of finding out the reasons and the ways of being an architect in a world whose symbols and heroes (old and new as well), for a long series of very good reasons, the students had totally refused. The students were in fact concerned about a different way of doing architecture for the building of a different world (we know what world we are talking about, but for clarity's sake we can say: not classist, not racist, not violent, not repressive, not alienating, not specializing, not unifying).[1]

Against this background one views the present state of architectural education. There is a restlessness among students although the reasons for this may vary from country to country. In India, this air of irrelevancy about the schools of architecture is, I believe, due to what may be called a crisis in the schools of architecture. At the root of this crisis is the inability of the profession to distinguish between skill acquisition and education, and to see that both are essential in some measure in the making of an architect. This has always been recognized throughout history and in all cultures. Vitruvius mentions this at the beginning of his treatise in the first century:

> Architects who have aimed at acquiring manual skills without scholarship have never been able to reach a position of authority to correspond to their pains, while those who relied only upon theories and scholarship were obviously hunting the shadow, not the substance. But those who have a thorough knowledge of both, like men armed at all points, have the sooner attained their object and carried authority with them.[2]

Similarly, while specifying the desired qualities of an architect, *Mayamatam*, the ancient Indian treatise on architecture too asks that the architect be well versed in all forms of knowledge; स्थपतिः स्थापनार्हः स्यात् सर्वशास्त्र विशारदः [*Sanskrit*].[3]

This requires co-existence of specialized training and liberal education, instrumental knowledge and critical inquiry. The former requires the school to be supportive of the society while the latter demands it take an adversarial position. While the schools in India have accepted, unquestioningly, the professional values as academically relevant and their role in producing young architects who can readily be absorbed into the existing framework of professional practice, those values have increasingly come to be recognized as extensions of the professional establishments. Most schools in India nurture syllabi that are heavily weighted in favor of technical and professional expertise, in the process neglecting to develop a learning environment that can generate a sense of inquiry and expose students to the relationships between architectural decisions and the cultural, moral and ethical predisposition of the decision maker. Such relationships have always existed in history and to understand them is the first prerequisite step toward an understanding of the nature of architectural activity.

It is becoming increasingly obvious that the sub-structural elements of civilized life, that is, the web of social, economic and political relationships of a community, the rhythm and patterns of habitation and a culture's sense of the relationship of humans to the world around them are inseparably linked to its superstructure, the physical environment of cities, buildings and landscapes. This linkage is often dialectical in the sense that the superstructure, by determining the disposition of activities in space and by erecting symbols of values in space, determines the nature of human relationships involved in these activities. At the same time, the nature of the physical environment is determined by the existing order of these relationships.

Thus the seemingly technical nature of architectural activity is not value-free and ethically neutral, and the sense of reality, truth and beauty, far from being universal and pre-determinable, is culturally variable. A school of architecture will be abdicating its responsibility if, in addition to technical and managerial proficiency, it fails to inculcate in young architects a habit of critical thinking with which to evaluate the dialectical relationship between the forces of change and their own technical and aesthetic decisions. This is especially critical in a developing and changing society such as India where the superstructural symbols an architect creates, whether they be detached houses for families, places of work or worship, or monuments, will tell of the chosen relationships between human and human, between humans and society and between society and nature.

The program and the method with which our schools educate and train young architects are derived from the idea of architecture we have inherited from the last three centuries of modernist discourse, which is increasingly being questioned as we shall see below. At the same time, the profession too is by and large geared towards perpetuating this discourse. Hence, if the future of the profession is to be negotiated in the schools, the programs and methods need more structural changes and not just superfluous tweaking of a course or schedule.

I want to introduce here three notions which might help us take the above to its logical conclusion. The first one is philosophical in nature and proposes a general way of thinking. I call this *Contingent Criticality*. The adjective *contingent* is meant to locate criticality in a contextual space. Criticality implies an objective and universal position and has been one of the foundations of the modernist project which celebrated the autonomous individual possessing a rationality disengaged from any contextual encumbrances. With this universalistic and ahistorical posture of modernism now being increasingly questioned, it is necessary that we reevaluate its underlying assumptions.

The Cartesian heritage, elaborated and extended by Kant, gave us this notion of reason as the *First Principle*, an abstract ideal, an immutable something through which everything can be judged but which itself cannot be scrutinized. Because reason in its transcendental form is disengaged, it has to be the same everywhere, in any culture. Culture, heritage or the material practices of people cannot ever mediate its intensions; it is dismissive of culture and context. Criticality thus assumes the Archimedean posture of being outside and independent of the telos of life itself and becomes universal. All the theoretical constructs of modern science as well as art are founded on this. From the Renaissance onward, the aesthetic ideal of the West has been to see life steadily and to see it whole; as an order rather than as a process, as complete within itself rather than as becoming, evolving, in the making.

That possibility of seeing life as a whole is one of the first casualties of our time not only because of the increasing velocity of history but also because of the realization that there is more than one way of looking at the world. Seeing life at once steadily and as a whole requires that the artist and their environment have a stable relationship over time. But when the artist found themself traveling, so to speak, at a thousand miles an hour across a landscape constantly taking new forms and colors, when time changed from an unexamined assumption into an interfering force, it became no longer possible to see life steadily and as a whole. W.B. Yeats said it well: "Things fall apart; the centre cannot hold."[4]

The search for techniques expressive of the fragmentation wrought by the increasing acceleration of life characterizes much of modern architecture as it does much of modern painting, music, sculpture and literature. Unfortunately, it accepts as its basis an assumption that, in the words of Peter Eisenman, "disharmony might be part of the cosmology that we live in" and that "the role of art and architecture might just be to remind people that everything is not all right."[5] In other words, in a fragmented world, nothing can be anchored or theoretically grounded and therefore "anything goes" is alright.

I, for one, want to reject this proposition. Cartesian thought has had a tendency to view the world in terms of stark polarities. Thus the opposite of critical would be uncritical and that of rational would be irrational. It is this polarity inherent in the Cartesian worldview and the implicit values (positive/negative, desirable/undesirable, etc.) that has prevented us from looking at an alternative theoretical framework.

Rejection of the First Principle does not have to imply a rejection of the rigorous application of logic and reason. The answer lies not in replacing one kind of "first principle" with another kind, as Eisenman's reference to cosmology seems to suggest. The obstacle, I think, is far more structural and requires us to locate architecture not in the realm of being (as autonomous buildings) but in the process of *becoming*, as events. For, if grounded in temporality of the event, the First Principle dissolves itself, as does the dichotomy of subject–object. Accepted as such, architecture's objective shifts from making autonomous buildings alone (although of course that is not to be undervalued) to creating situations in which life on this planet can unfold itself. In other words, it is a continuously evolving action and as such it is aimed at creating places for people; places that are appropriate to and supportive of their situation; places that respond to human need, stir the imagination and, at their best, dignify human existence; and above all places that inform the discourse about what places are and what they should be.

Thus architecture is a value-loaded activity. An architect is obliged to question what might be appropriate or supportive of the situation and, at the same time, to be aware of the implicit values of the society, which might support (or be likely to oppose) a particular design decision. This action has to be constantly validated and revalidated not by any abstract First Principle but by the material, intellectual and ethical context within which it is taken. Thus the action is *critical* to the extent that it is deliberate and willful (as opposed to habitual), but this criticality is also relative and *contingent* upon its context. This context is not limited to the physical location of the event but would encompass genuinely plural worldviews.

We thus arrive at a brief outline of an alternative theoretical framework that is inclusive enough to justify the immense diversity and multiplicity of life around us and at the same time rigorous enough to guard against the anarchy of the seductive image as well as the dictatorship of the preferred few. It not only encompasses the work of an architect as a professional but also the pedagogical considerations of the school, which brings me to the other two notions that I want to introduce.

The second notion is *Concerned Making*. Here the adjective *concerned* seeks to bring an ethical and moral dimension to the act of making, that is, of putting together something. By "concerned" I mean that our architects will not only be aware of their given situation but also care enough about it to want to change it. In other words, we aim to produce not only architects as technicians/ designers but also architects as citizens. *Making* involves all the necessary technical competencies and aesthetic sensibilities required for the production of the built environment: the art of putting together a building well. However, over the years this has acquired a technological bias and the consideration of quality and the nature of the elements has been forgotten. But technology is also not free of ideological considerations. Making also involves making choices between technologies whose consequences are not always properly evaluated. Thus available technologies must, in all situations, be weighed against their appropriateness in a given situation. The school will seek to equip students with the understanding of their own society and the world around them necessary to be able to bridge the gap between technological considerations and their ethical and aesthetic dimensions. Thus *Concerned Making*. I believe that nature, in the forms of landscape, climate and its laws of material and construction, is an important partner in the making of architecture. The term *Concerned Making* seeks to foster a reverence both for nature as well as for our fellow beings.

The third idea introduces a method of practicing architecture, which is in tune with both *Contingent Criticality* and *Concerned Making*. I call this *Reflective Action*.

Most professional schools of architecture structure the overall program so that students first learn a set of "the basics" of architecture a the given representational and conceptual tools, the formal and constructional conventions and principles of how architecture goes together, what are considered "good" practices and so on before they are asked to question anything. It has almost become a conventional wisdom that one must learn the basic language before one expresses anything. This legacy of the Bauhaus remains with all the so-called "Basic Design" or "Foundation Program" components of the pedagogy.

The underlying assumption here is that a person's maturity is skill-based. The acquisition of skill and the ability to handle more and more complex tasks is considered an indication of increased maturity. This has resulted in all our schools starting with the basic tools and then increasing the complexities in later stages with advancing years. It is assumed that as maturity increases so will a person's inclination to question the validity of the tools and the skills they have been given.

I question this basic premise. I believe that the methods (tools and skills) of observation and communication limit the phenomena to be observed and communicated. Thus the tools and skills of design acquired in the early years limit a student's ability to explore the range of possibilities to only those accessible with these particular tools and skills.

Maturity is not skill-based. Maturity is a person's ability to come to terms with their own capacities and limitations. Skills change as the technologies (tools) change, and will be acquired as needed and appropriate. A school's pedagogy cannot be based on skills, which can soon become outdated. It must be founded on exploration and students' coming to terms with what they are doing and why.

Almost all our high schools, and the family, have taught us to think before doing anything. Thinking through anything prior to doing has become second nature. But in architecture the sequential relationship between thinking and doing is often reversed; in fact it is so in all creative disciplines. An architect often explores through a sketch or a model (an action) and then ponders (thinks) about its consequences. Doing precedes thinking.

The program, at least in the initial semesters, should aspire to start at the point where basic insights are developed by doing design, even ineptly at first, in order to discover for oneself what can be done, what are the potentials of designing inhabited space, and in order to find one's own questions about what ought to be proposed. In other words, we intend to put the fundamental premise of the studio, "learning by doing," into practice.

This would initially challenge students to explore a number of possibilities, without prior authorization of the directions favored by the faculty or by their conscious intellect. Judgment as to the suitability of any of these proposals will have to come after, not before, the range and diversity of possibilities they have produced within the limits of a given situation have been exhausted. In other words, the process begins with the question: "What ought one to do in this situation here and now, that one can support, and why?" This will have to be done after there are several actual design proposals in front of the student for interrogation, and not before. This certainly is going to result in a lengthy and not unlikely confusing initial program. But we will have to deal with this.

I call this *Reflective Action*. By this I mean a design action taken in response to a well-considered critical evaluation of its suitability and supportability in a given situation. This is opposed to habitual action or action which may be seen as in vogue at the time.

In conclusion, the elements required for the crucial mix that will make the school of architecture relevant again are thus emerging more clearly from the above. They range from an abstraction such as the self-image of the school to concrete curricular changes. The schools of architecture must recognize and acknowledge the difference between architecture and the profession of architecture. Strange as it may seem, they often do not share the same values and may also be working at cross purposes and harboring conflicting interests. Although it is not necessary to take sides, it must be recognized that the schools are supported by the society at large, whose interests, in terms of the quality of built environments, they must safeguard.

The schools of architecture must be interested in a ceaseless and wholesale critique of architecture at all times; a critique aimed not at a realignment of design with the problem of production, not even with the modes of social organization, but at an understanding of the architectural act itself. This will be the act of building shelters and monuments in the face of which nature and culture are to be recognized. This act will have to be defined neither in terms of the encounter between an architect and a client nor in terms of the capacity of a building form to convey certain programmatic purposes (both definitions so dear to the profession), but as an act of building initiated by people's need for shelter, sustained by the logic of construction and impregnated with meaning by the mythology rooted in the time and place of its making.

The intuitive and creative work done in the studios must be supported with critical thought. This must be done by making ideas that inform architecture a greater part of our professional preparation. History should be studied not as a sequence of facts, but rather as an experience related to those facts in their development, and theory not as abstract, immutable principles but as the structure and interpretation of those historical events as a system of reciprocal relationships in which every element, permanent or ephemeral, is in function with every other.

In short, the school must become a place where, for a student, all the morphological and structural conceptions and all the operational tools, which have thus far governed architecture, become open to question. A vast set of alternatives and variables, which the institutional culture and profession has suppressed, come back into play. Only under this condition can a student articulate and develop a clear ideological position and learn to take decisions, which derive their validity from their own, clearly formulated intentions.

Notes

1 Giancarlo De Carlo, "Legitimizing Architecture," *Forum*, 23(1) (1972), 9.
2 Vitruvius, *The Ten Books on Architecture*. Trans. Morris Hicky Morgan (New York: Dover Publications, 1960), 5.
3 Bruno Dagens (trans). *Mayamatam Treatise on Housing, Architecture and Lonography* (New Delhi: Motilal Banarasidas, 1994), 24–25.
4 W.B. Yeats, *The Second Coming* (1920).
5 P. Eisenman and C. Alexander, "The Debate: Contrasting Concepts of Harmony in Architecture," *Lotus International*, 40 (1983), 60–68.

Part Two
The Idea of Architecture

Chapter 5

Architecture and the Idea
of Agreement

It is indeed a privilege to speak at this gathering commemorating the memory of my dear friend and colleague Kurula Varkey.[1] I have now spent almost 40 years of my life engaged with this institution, 25 of these as an active faculty member. When I think about those years my memories revive a series of encounters—with people, with places, with situations and with ideas—which have mostly enriched my life in innumerable ways. Varkey was an important part of those memories.

So it is only appropriate that today we restate and reaffirm those ideas and values held dear by people like Kurula Varkey and which increasingly seem to be on trial today. One look at our cities will tell us that at its worst, today's world seems to be a world in which people are intent on setting their own rules. On the other hand, at its best, it is a world in which the discrepancies, the paradoxes and the rejections represent a way of relating oneself to events and, in doing so, acquiring an awareness of the multiple aspects of life. Nowadays, we architects are increasingly being pulled by these conflicting demands. We are either asked to adhere to the most pragmatic and utilitarian aspirations or expected to align our work with that which is in fashion today. The space for *good* architecture is fast shrinking.

In such conditions a multitude of questions flood the mind. How do we define and understand the activity we call architecture? What informs what we do? What do architects do and how does it differ from what others, say scientists, do? Why do we design? Has design a specific purpose in the life of all and not that of just a few. Just as scientific discovery makes us understand the underlying order in the manifest world of nature around us, does design serve a larger purpose? What do we mean when we say "I practice architecture"? Toward what end? Is it to make a living? Is it to be able to pay for our daily meals and for our children's education? Is it to build shelter for humankind or for the privileged few? How do I make my choices given a range of possible options? And so on.

One of the things that is easily noticed about architects, at least some of them, is that they are very passionate about their work and are often intolerant of any lapse in quality and poor execution. Sheer survival is not enough to explain the high level of passion and attachment for which some architects are known to single-mindedly pursue their goal.

What is that goal then? As for providing shelter to humankind, we certainly do contribute toward the creation of places of our accommodations: houses, schools, work places and hospitals. And of course, there is a degree of enjoyment in being able to fulfill this larger need of the society. But this enjoyment must come as a byproduct of something else which goes much deeper than the social obligation, which is utilitarian in nature and quite independent of the quest for quality and perfection that distinguishes an architect's work. If an architect worked mainly to fulfill a social obligation, which has its own rewards and many architects are passionately devoted to such work, this passion is qualitatively different from the passion for perfection. Indeed, I might even venture to say that one is mutually exclusive of the other. For an architect whose main aim is to fulfill a social obligation may tend to overlook any shortfall in quality, and this will be true the other way round too. We will have to look for the meaning of our work somewhere else.

At this juncture, I am tempted to describe to you a beautiful event I witnessed when I was young and one that may contain a hint of the answers we are seeking. It was a journey I undertook many years ago into lands that are far from here and antipodean and in many ways belonging to a different time, but not for that reason any less significant to us today. I am referring to the northern stretches of our country, the Himalayan wilderness of the northern provinces where the boundaries between solitude and togetherness are often indistinguishable. This journey, and the event I witnessed there, has been forever etched in my memory and it was only many years later, when I was struggling to find meaning in my work as an architect, that I came to realize its significance.

I had only been in the first year of my education as an architect when a young man in my class, whom I had befriended only a few months ago, invited me to spend, with his family in his ancestral village in the remote Gharwal hills in the northern provinces, the Diwali festival, the post-harvest festival of light and offering of thanks for the little mercies of God for which the farmer is always grateful.

His village was in that region where the rocky slopes of the mountains give way to the gentle plains and the turbulent white waters of the many adolescent rivers merge with, and acquire the quiet dignity of the mighty Ganga. Great primordial forests must have once occupied these hills which are now dwellings to people who still live with the ancient rites but are no less wise for that.

On the evening of Diwali, just before sundown, my friend said, "Come with me. I want to show you something." I had no idea what he wanted to show but he took me to the woods in the direction of the river where we had gone every morning since I had arrived and free of all care and concern had splashed for hours in the cold mountain waters of the holy river feeling invigorated and purified. But this evening my friend's face suggested that this youthful frivolity seemed to be far from the objective of our journey tonight.

We walked in silence. Each of us filled with our own solitude, increasingly being engulfed by the growing darkness of the moonless night, the only sound an occasional flutter of wings of a bird sensing the danger of unknown intrusion into their domain. It was a dazzling and secret world of nature at once stimulating but also menacing with growing cold and the fear of the unknown. Everything became one: the solitude, the danger, the silence and the anticipation of what I did not know.

We continued till we came to the end of the thick woods. I could sense the presence of the river somewhere ahead though I had not been to this particular place before. I suppose it must have been the feel of the ground below my feet; it had turned hard and rocky and its gentle slope propelled me, with an unfamiliar insistence, to keep moving. In this darkness I had the strange sensation that my whole body was alive and that I was one with my surroundings. Now, after many years, when I think back to that moment I realize that, though not by design on the part of my friend, but still by bringing me here in this quiet way, anticipation having taken me to the edge of my senses, the circumstances had conspired, in a strange way, to prepare me for what was to follow.

I was shaken out of my introspection when my friend put his hand on my shoulder and said, "Can you hear it?" Sure enough, from the direction of the village we had left behind, came a faint sound of singing.

"Are they dancing?" I asked.

"No. Listen carefully" my friend said. No, they were not dancing. Their song did not have the exuberance and the joyful abandon of young dancers. Instead it was somber and devotional. And besides, the sound seemed to be coming nearer and nearer to where we were.

We sat on a high boulder and waited. In the distance I could see, across the valley, the dark silhouette of the distant hills with the occasional flicker of light coming from scattered settlements on their slopes. The river, though shrouded in darkness, must have been down there somewhere.

We must have waited for almost ten minutes before the singers were close enough for us to understand what they were singing. Theirs was a song of praise and of gratitude, of the plentiful rains they have received and the sunshine and of love and good health. It was a song of joy. All the villagers, adults and children, singing in unison, were moving in a procession toward the river. Each of them had, in their right palm, a small earthen bowl containing vegetable oil and a cotton string which was lit on one end forming a lamp not dissimilar to the lamps which had decorated their houses and their forecourts. In the warm glow of their own lamps one could see their faces full of love and joy. Their singing was accompanied by several pairs of brass cymbals and a drum producing a percussion sound that filled the air.

Suddenly, I also saw other similar processions of light and sound in the distant hills. Soon the hills were all lit up in the warm glow of tiny lights and the sound filled the valley. All seemed to be converging on both banks of the holy river.

Shortly, they all arrived at the river. Their singing had reached a crescendo. The cymbals and the drums were now beating a feverish rhythm. Everyone seemed to be in a trance. I could identify with them for like me they too had become part of their surroundings. Each of them had willingly merged their individual identities with the togetherness of the group and with the poetry of the event.

As if on a signal they started to form a single line facing the river. Soon there were two strings of light each stretching almost a kilometer on both banks of the river. Suddenly the river came alive. Its calm water, a mirror-like expanse, reflected the lights on the opposite bank. I became conscious of the flow of the water and realized that now the song was gentler, its rhythm and modulation matching the flow of the water.

Without a break in the song the people bent over and set the lamps afloat on the water. Hundreds of tiny specks of light filled the river and gently started moving downstream. The song continued in the same rhythm matching the flow of water. The song, the light and the river had all become one. The river was set on fire by the generous offering of life back to the giver of life.

Ladies and gentlemen, it was not to seduce you by its poetry and exoticness that I recounted, in such great detail, a past event, etched in my memory for ever, in a land so far and so different from the one we are occupying tonight. I did this because I believe in that dark night, lit by life itself, I sensed an important element of my work as an architect. I say "sensed" because only recently, many years later, that sense is beginning to form what might be called an insight, which I may or may not be able to articulate in my work and words, but which will certainly make me realize something about myself.

I believe, in that simple ceremony, the inhabitants of the Gharwal hills were engaged in an act of design; an act (and all art is action) which was more than a mere transformation of nature into culture. It was an unmistakable sublimation, a word almost forgotten from our lexicon. A sublimation of the daily experiences of being in that particular location; of going to the river every day, experiencing the gentle but firm flow of the water, looking across the valley and sensing the solidarity of a shared community, of illuminating one's evenings with the flickering lamp. But above all it was the sublimation in which all distinctions between art and life became meaningless and in which there joined as equal partners humans and nature.

The design of that ceremony was not aimed at any exigency of the moment. Nor was it to provide a solution to the inhabitants' daily problems. It did not in any way materially enrich them or ease the drudgery of labor. But it did dignify human existence and to me it informed the nature of that place, the nature of the people living in that place and the nature of human construct, be it a simple ceremony, a poem or a building, in a way that no description, not even this of my own, could possibly ever do.

Many years later, and far from the solitude of the Gharwal hills, when I was in Philadelphia preoccupied with more immediate concerns of building productions, I came across a quotation from L.B. Alberti with which, had they been as articulate as Alberti, the people of the Gharwal hills would certainly have agreed. It says: "Arts were begot by chance and observation and nursed by use and experience and improved and perfected by reason and study."[2] This observation by Alberti has the simplicity of truth. You see, Alberti was an architect, among many other things, who believed architecture to be an example of an art as a way of life. In fact, he went through the pains of writing about architecture, not making theories but condensing and sublimating, not unlike the people of the Gharwal hills, the experience of ten centuries before him: he was looking for laws, the laws which set limits to architecture. Too often theory presupposes the absence of experience; it is believed to transcend experience. The finding of a law is instead the sublimation of experience. Alberti was looking for those laws which precede and determine the individual choices of an artist without which no freedom is possible. Alberti believed architecture to be an art not distinct from life.

Nowadays, we avoid, as much as possible, talking of architecture as an art. We either feel shy about the word, or have lost the sense of its meaning, or worse, we think altogether that architecture is not an art but some kind of clever making, even happening.

But I believe this only partially answers the questions we started out with. How do we understand the nature of the activity we call architecture? There is still something not quite clear. One of the most perceptive and elegant thinkers of our time, Hannah Arendt, has come up with a beautiful formulation of an idea which may show us the way forward. Relying on the rich tradition of Western thought, and especially the classical Greek thought, she has classified all human activities into three broad categories of Labor, Work and Action, and has given us a radical new way of looking at our work. Let us briefly examine each of Hannah Arendt's three categories and see where we can locate architecture.

Labor, according to this formulation, constitutes all activities of humans that are propelled by the necessity of sheer survival, and is located at the lowest rung in the hierarchy of all human activities. Thus, labor is motivated by a compulsion for survival. It is not an act of human will exercised in freedom by free individuals who alone, according to Greek thought, have a right to be referred to as humans. Also labor does not produce anything of lasting presence. What labor produces from the material taken from nature goes back to nature without leaving any traces. For example, the product of the human labor of transporting something from one place to another does not produce anything. Or the labor of a baker, who makes a loaf of bread but has only a transient presence until the bread is consumed. It does not add to the lasting value that constitutes the world around us. Even Karl Marx, who defined humans as *animal laborans,* had to admit that the productivity of labor, properly speaking, begins only with reification, with the erection of the objective world of things.

Work, the second category, on the other hand, produces durable things that constitute the human-made world. This human-made world, the home erected on earth and made of the material which nature has given to humans, consists not of things that are consumed but of things that are used.

Thus it is the end product that distinguishes labor and work. While the laboring human is referred to as *animal laborans*, the working human is referred to as *homo faber,* the fabricator. Fabrication, the work of *homo faber*, consists of reification, that is, giving a concrete presence to an idea. It is the work of human hands that takes raw materials from nature and transforms them into new forms through the process of making. Unlike the objects of consumption—the products of labor—the things of this world are characterized by their relative durability, which makes them independent of, and outlive, humans who produce them and use them. The fabricating process, in fact, is entirely distinct and independent from the fabricated thing itself. And it is this independence of the fabricated object that gives it its duration and the "thing"-like character without which we would not have the human-made world which mediates between humans and nature.

Unlike the two categories of labor and work, where Miss Arendt identifies humans as either *animal laborans* or *homo faber*, respectively, she does not provide a singular label for the third category: action. In fact this emerges as a multi-faceted category with thought, contemplation and speech, as well as action, as distinct initiatives, being considered in great detail. However, in the end she narrows it down to "speech and action," two interdependent functions, as truly human actions.

This third category also differs from the earlier two in one very important way. While both labor and work can be performed by individuals alone, speech and action requires the presence of others. In fact, plurality is an essential precondition for speech and action. Both are directed at others and are founded on the fact that each individual is a distinct and unique being. It is this distinctness that is being expressed and communicated through speech and actions. It is evident, then, that the existence of the public realm is essential for this to happen; on the public realm can humans appear and express themselves through speech and action.

The outcome of both speech and action, in their most evolved form is unpredictable. This alludes to the spontaneous and un-predetermined character of all creative actions. This is contrary to the conventional wisdom that one should know beforehand what one is saying or doing. This may be true of a fabricator, who has an idea (a mental image or a drawing or a model) of what they are making. But for someone who is undertaking a new initiative, the outcome is unpredictable. This unpredictability is related to the revelatory, or one should say self-revelatory, character of a creative act. It not only reveals, at the end, the nature of the action but also discloses the individual's self without them ever knowing themself.

What is abundantly clear from the above is the unmistakable convergence between this ancient Greek thought and the equally ancient Indian thought, as expressed in *Gita*, regarding the actions of humans—that the innermost meaning of the acted deed and the spoken word is independent of result and must remain untouched by any eventual outcome, by their consequences for better or worse.

Let me quote Hannah Arendt verbatim to end this brief and rather simplified reference to her startling and penetrating study of modern humans.

> [E]ach individual in his unique distinctness appears and confirms himself in speech and action, and that these activities, despite their material futility, possess an enduring quality of their own because they create their own *remembrance*. The public realm, the space within the world which men need in order to appear at all, is therefore *more specifically "the work of man" than is the work of his hands or the labor of his body.*[3]
>
> (italics mine)

Thus, it is the creation of this very public realm—"institution" as Kahn referred to it—which is the end product of speech and action.

(Here Miss Arendt follows and reaffirms the Cartesian/Kantian legacy of the mind–body duality: Humans are defined away from their bodies. I do not fully endorse it. But for our present purpose, we shall temporarily suspend our disagreement and continue.)

The above formulation by a philosopher does give us a much broader and comprehensive conceptual framework with which to return to our inquiry regarding the nature and meaning of architecture and to answer the questions we started out with. We have already noted that the work of an architect is often propelled by a passionate urge, no different than that of the people of the Gharwal hills, to communicate to the rest of us a sense of order, and the oneness, "*advitiam*" (non-duality) in the world around us. This, then, locates architecture within the category of speech and action in Miss Arendt's scheme of things. This would mean that architecture, like speech and action, is ephemeral and has no material presence. But this is contrary to the conventional notion of architects as the makers of the human-made world, buildings and cities, around us. How do we resolve this apparent contradiction? We will be forgiven if we think of ourselves as fabricators—*homo fabers*. But then architecture is universally considered a creative act; an act that brings about a new initiative. In ancient India too even though architects have been referred to as *Vishvakarma*—the maker of the world—they always have been accorded a status much higher than that given to artisans, the "*Shilpi*" (craftsmen).

I believe we can resolve this if we define architecture as an idea. Let us say that architecture is an idea that is embodied in the building. The building then is the courier that carries the idea of architecture. But that begs several crucial questions. Are all buildings architecture? If they are all couriers of the idea of architecture, what do you make of the incredible variety we see in our cities today? And if not, what will inform the distinction? The above may suggest that the work of an architect is informed by their very subjective being; that it is their idea and their desire to communicate this idea that propels them and helps them make their decisions. In other words, anything goes. I, for one, reject this simple conclusion. Unlike the work of *animal laboran* and the *homo faber*, the work of an architect, if it resides in the realm of speech and action, happens in the public realm.

This implies that, far from being a subjective act whose validity lies only in the private reasoning of the individual architect, architecture is a public act. A public act can come about and has a chance of being sustained as an integral part of the public domain only if it has received an express or tacit agreement from others. Acceptance of the idea of architecture in the public realm is a precondition for the durability of architecture. It is rooted in the time and place of its making and derives its meaning through this rootedness.

Still, our cities today are indeed chaotic, disorderly and visually "noisy." One may be forgiven for thinking that there is no agreement and that architects are simply exercising their free will. We are tempted to think of this as only a reflection of the fragmentary nature of the times we live in. That is why many of us yearn for earlier times when things were more predictable and great cultures evolved.

But apart from the apparent absence of cultural agreement, there is still another level at which architecture must be seen as being not only a subjective and personal statement of the architect. The physical body of architecture, the building, once erected, becomes a part not only of the human-made world but also of nature and must then follow the laws of nature as is true of the entire objective world. The world erected by *homo faber* may have given humans an illusion that they, with their ability to erect an alternative world, can also control and rule over nature. However, it would be a folly to ascribe an adversarial and mutually antagonistic relationship between the two worlds. We may take a clue from what Louis I. Kahn has said: "Man is made of nature but is not nature." This suggests a rather complex relationship between humans and nature whereby while humans have the capacity to think and do what nature cannot, at the same time what they make with their hands and bodies (as opposed to what they think and imagine) must be done in cooperation with nature and within the objective laws that govern all things.

These two in-built regulatory mechanisms, that is, agreement or being culturally rooted and adherence to the laws of nature, one cultural and the other natural, prevent architecture from falling in that pit where "anything goes." Its genesis may be located in the deep psyche of the architect and as such it has no presence until it finds an embodiment in the building which is an offering in the public realm and as such can be sustained only if it has cultural validity and it is built within the laws of nature.

The validity of architecture, then, relies on three variables; one, the desire of the architect to express an idea, or the force or inevitability of an idea to find expression; two, the agreement amongst the architect's fellow citizens in the society; and three, the cooperation of nature, either in the form of the materials it provides or its laws within which the medium of expression—building—has to be offered to the public domain. Out of these three only the last, nature and its laws, can be said to be relatively constant and the agreement the most complex to understand.

The "agreement" is also the least predictable of the three variables for it involves finding a common denominator among a multitude of human psyches. For that very reason it is also a very fickle and short-lived, transient phenomenon. In its most ideal state, the agreement permeates the entire culture. It encompasses the multiple relationships between humans, humans and nature, humans and society, and society and nature in tune with each other and internalized by all. Such an all-encompassing agreement manifests itself in all cultural productions, be they literature, architecture, music or simple ceremonies on the banks of river Ganga.

But we do not live in such an ideal time; in fact, such idyllic cultural conditions are a rarity. As such it is easy for the agreement to descend to the world of fashion where it can be, without much difficulty, manipulated or manufactured. It is the objective of the modern advertising profession to artificially "manufacture" a social agreement by making an object or a design desirable or a general perception of it being desirable. In fact the transient nature of the object is a necessary condition in such a situation and is often built into the fashion agreement: the loss of the use value and the disintegration of the aura or the patina of the object is a precondition of the market economy. There is also a contemporary name for it: "planned obsolescence" whereby not only the end of the object but also the end of the desire for it is planned in its conception. Obviously, under these conditions, a building whose design is founded on what may be in vogue, or fashionable at the time of its making may only be a short-lived object of consumption and therefore neither the work of *home faber* nor that of the *homo communicator*. Such buildings may not be included in the category of architecture.

On the other hand, when a stable and long-lasting agreement exists, architecture lends an unmistakable identity, an aura to the society and its culture. Thus when we refer to a period in history as, say, Greco-Roman, Gothic, Renaissance or Gupta period in India, we imply that throughout that period an agreement prevailed about the language of architecture and the system of its construction. There existed an underlying consensus about what constitutes the spirit of that society and its values and the architecture that expressed it. A few of these buildings do it better than the others and still a few others may break new grounds and may herald the arrival of a new agreement, a new worldview and a new era. Such buildings transcend the durational boundaries of their own time and attain timelessness. We call them "classics."

The Crystal Palace (Figure 2.2) was one such classic work of architecture. Joseph Paxton not only captured and expressed the spirit of its time but also pointed toward a new spatial conception and a new way to build it. While the building is no more, it has left behind a "lasting remembrance" (to quote Hannah Arendt). Its expression was inevitable: had it not been Paxton, someone else would have built it, maybe differently. In the early 1960s, the British group, Archigram, had already sensed dissatisfaction with the orthodoxies of the modern movement and had proposed alternatives with their visionary images. The work of this avant-garde group was initially seen more as a curiosity, though it did help crystallize an agreement that ultimately made it possible for Richard Rogers and Renzo Piano's Pompidou Center to be received favorably (Figure 5.1).

Figure 5.1
Centre Georges-Pompidou from Notre-Dame de Paris. Renzo Piano, Richard Rogers and Gianfranco Franchini, Paris, 1971–1977.

But then could the timelessness of the Crystal Palace imply that it could have been built by the Greeks in the fifth century BC or during the Middle Ages? Conversely, could we build the Parthenon or Reims Cathedral, both of them timeless works, today and call them architecture? The material and intellectual conditions in Greece and during the Middle Ages will not have given birth to or supported the Crystal Palace. And only under two conditions can we conceive of building the Parthenon or Reims Cathedral today; at best as a quotation within a larger work, as a semiotic statement to make a point, like many of the Greek revival façades on the nineteenth-century banks; or at worst as a fashion statement, as an object of desire or a commodity of consumption. In either case they will lie outside the realm of architecture in the true sense.

Obviously we are confronted with a plurality of conceptions (agreements) about architecture throughout history. Architecture has always been reinterpreted, reinvented and its objective redefined to arrive at an agreement that is in harmony with the prevailing material and intellectual culture of the society. However, there has also been a core belief in the ultimate validity of architecture that has remained and survived the plurality and the historical progression. This we have not yet articulated.

This core belief, I believe, must be found beyond history and evolution. It must be located in those moments when the work of *homo faber*—the utilitarian and mechanical structures that constitute the built world around us—was transformed and elevated from the mundane to the sublime. This transformation also, at the same time, transformed humans from mere fabricators to *communicators*. With this humans had crossed that line separating the realm of labor and work and found their "speech and action."

This happened in all cultures and civilizations. Let us imagine a possible scenario. As agrarian people began to settle down and build shelter for their numerous needs such as houses, places of worship, storage of grains and so on their initial attempts were simple and direct responses to the forces of nature and made with whatever material they could gather from the surrounding nature. This must have gone on for several generations—centuries, even—and extended across many different communities. During this time each builder not only repeated the task as their ancestors had performed it, but also observed others around them. They faced the problem of building foundations, erecting walls of stones or posts from tree trunks and, probably the most complex task of all, building the roof with solutions that not only provided protection from the weather but also dealt with the problem of gravity.

Repeating the tasks again and again, observing each other doing it differently, gradually coming to terms with the nature of each task and how each material behaved seems to have led to the acceptance by the entire community that some solutions are better suited to the situation than others. These agreed-upon building methods spread to other communities in the region facing similar problems and must have been internalized over generations. These formed part of the tradition carrying the accumulated wisdom of the society. These building solutions became the repository of the collective memory and the knowledge of people. Everyone recognized and accepted them.

Here we have the first level of agreement, commonly referred to as *tradition*. This may have given rise to a group of master craftsmen with the authority to interpret the community's building needs and provide appropriate solutions. Through rigorous and constant practice these master craftsmen had made the craft of building their second nature and in due course some of them created buildings that not only had perfected the traditional ways of building the various elements of a house or a temple, but in their very arrangement of the parts and in their relationship with the world around them represented the order of the universe as they perceived it and made others also sense it. These buildings acquired iconic status. Everyone looked at these buildings in awe and must have nodded their head in agreement.

At this point these buildings had truly left behind the initial utilitarian reasons that had brought them about in the first place. Those reasons still remained and the buildings continued to play their assigned roles of being houses, temples or granaries, but there was something sublime about them that made us sense reality deeply by making us take a critical stance vis-à-vis that reality. This was done not by mimicking the reality but by re-presenting it, not only as it existed but also as it could be. In other words, these buildings embodied the idea of architecture. At this moment they became architecture.

This phenomenon is independent of history and geography. It is true of the Parthenon as much as it is true of the Crystal Palace. These buildings point toward the essential duality of the act of architecture and tell us of an inseparable relationship between the idea of architecture and the craft of building, the mind of humans and their hands and bodies. One resides in the realm of the cerebral while the other in the sensual and the experiential. Together, they represent the totality of architecture. Their relationship is neither hierarchical nor sequential. And above all, it overcomes the mind–body duality: it incorporates speech and action but also the work of *homo faber*.

Much of the world's great architecture is the result of this process. The real contact with architecture and with the architect is made, then, beyond learned expressions of aesthetic styles, when the substance of humans' existence as individuals and as a community is simply but uncompromisingly stated. This does not occur simply because a formal synthesis is obtained, but rather because a comprehensive idea of architecture is validated. It happened in a simple barn in the middle of an American farm, or in the Mexican haçienda or in an Indian haweli. And for sure it was present when the people of the Gharwal hills evolved that simple ceremony of thanksgiving.

However, the simple certainty, which resulted in these examples, is no longer obtainable today. Let me end by repeating what I said at the beginning. At its worst, today's world seems to be one in which people are intent on setting their own rules. Much of our present urban landscape prompts one to question the very idea of an agreement; there does not seem to be any. On the other hand, at its best, it is a world in which the discrepancies, the paradoxes and the rejections represent a way of relating oneself to events and, in so doing, acquiring an awareness of the multiple aspects of life. It is tempting to want to return to an earlier time when a simpler and more immediately comprehensible order obtained. But that would amount to denying the history that has brought us here and making time itself an adversary.

Today's architects, as a consequence, is also bound to the destiny of their society and its institutions, not unlike the master builders of the past, even though they may at times appear as an individual enjoying what may be only an illusory freedom. Their role is in living the process of events and taking upon themself the great risk of realizing the conjectures and the possibilities of that society: in particular, realizing the link between infinite nature and finite humans.

Thus, the architect is willing and capable of taking that risk for a better and more conscious world, fully knowing that its future must be painstakingly built upon the present. In this they are forever engaged in articulating the agreement. If architects are authors, they are authors not only of their buildings but, and this is more significant, also of the agreement that revalidates the comprehensive idea of architecture. That can be the only precondition for the authenticity of a work of architecture today. If we can achieve it, who knows, we may still build cathedrals that are white.

Notes

1 This chapter was first delivered as the "Kurula Varkey Memorial Lecture" at CEPT University, Ahmedabad, 2014.

2 As conveyed to the author by Romaldo Giurgola, Philadelphia, 1974.

3 Hannah Arendt, *The Human Condition* (Chicago: University of Chicago Press, 1958), 207–208.

Chapter 6

The Space of Mr. Giedion

In the early 1950s and 1960s I grew up as a young student of architecture and developed my own understanding of architectural space after reading Sigfried Giedion's sweeping essay "Space, Time and Architecture,"[1] which attempted to present a coherent and universal spatial theory for the modern movement in architecture. These decades were marked by a sense of certitude about the direction architecture was taking. In this book, which was first published in 1941, Giedion had attempted the most coherent theoretical framework and an agenda for the emerging architecture. The publication of this book must have been one of those epochal moments in the history of architecture when an established epistemological paradigm gets thoroughly displaced to be replaced by a new revolutionary way of thinking. For a very long time, architectural knowledge, and its history, was built around the architectural object, its corporeal qualities and its iconography. Space was not even a part of our lexicon, except in academia. Giedion introduced us to the concept of space as an important element of architecture and presented us with a coherent narrative and a thoroughly convincing argument to explain the almost revolutionary architecture that was happening all around us. It brought architecture on a par with the developments in science, philosophy and other plastic arts. His time span for this study was the last 200 years during which the ideological foundation of modern architecture was laid. But his reference was much deeper and wider, which became clear a few years later when Giedion followed this up with another well-researched book but this time on ancient Egyptian architecture.[2] More than two millennia separated the two focuses of his inquiry and though this demonstrated the vast intellectual breadth of the author, it was initially baffling.

Still, there was a clear plan and a hint of it was given at the very beginning of the second book when the author wrote, "The study of continuity helps to elucidate the problems of change, which *contains the seeds of future development*. . . . The position and the development of architecture are linked to the new dimensions"[3] (italics mine). This intention to look for continuity and the seeds for future development became explicit in the last 30 pages of the book, which were devoted to an exploration of "Architectural Space Conception." It was clear that Giedion was looking for the historical source, the fountainhead, as it were, of the rational and relativist space conception of the twentieth century, which was the theme of the first book. There was also another agenda, far more profound and far-reaching; that of looking for a *universal theory of space* that would transcend all civilizational and cultural variations and nuances in the history of architecture.

Toward this end, Giedion proposed a three-stage progressive development of space conception. He located the first stage in Egypt and Greece as characterized by "abstraction, the supremacy of the vertical, the plane surface, volume in space" (p. 502). A few pages later, he makes an interesting statement that makes his position clear:

> Both the pyramids of Giza and the Acropolis at Athens express a similar relation to inner and outer space. Neither the Greeks nor the Egyptians ever developed interior space with the same intensity they expanded on relating their architecture to the cosmos.
>
> (p. 521)

What is implied here is that space as an enclosure to be inhabited by humans was not yet comprehended by humans, and their conception of space was limited to articulating and organizing the exterior space by positioning their architecture as an objective presence and not as an inhabited place. The sense of interiority of space was yet to emerge in this narrative of progressive historical development.

The second stage of the development of space conception, according to Giedion, is attributed to the Roman period:

> Interior space, and with it the whole vaulting problem, became the highest aim of architecture. In the space conception of the second stage, the notion of architectural space was almost identical with the notion of hollowed-out interior space. From late antiquity onwards hollowed-out space—circumscribed interior space—was the finest achievement of the art of building.
>
> (p. 521)

Giedion proposed that the key elements of both the first and the second stages of space conception are contained in the third stage, which, not being preoccupied exclusively with either the exterior space (first stage) or interior space (second stage), aimed to collapse this rigid polarity into a single expression in which the clear distinction between the exterior and the interior was replaced by a space that was at once neither and yet both. Space is no more an objective "thing" with boundaries but a progressive concentration of energy brought about by planer surfaces. Mies van der Rohe's hypothetical project of Brick Country House (1923), which was followed by the German Pavilion at Barcelona (1929) and Frank Lloyd Wright's Robie House (1909) are classic examples of this.

This is a neat formulation and has the power of simplicity and Hegelian inevitability. No wonder it quickly gained currency and became the received wisdom during the first half of the twentieth century. However, upon closer examination one finds it problematic on several counts. First, while the author claims, at several places in the book, the universal applicability of his theory of space in architecture, it is founded on the experiences of the Western civilization only. A universal theory implies that there is a singular theory that can incorporate and explain the conceptions of space of all the civilizations of the world. Such a position has no room for a plurality of conceptions responding to the different experiences of different civilizations and cultures. If theory is a sublimation of experience, a theory claiming to be universal must take into consideration experiences of other high civilizations such as the Indian and Persian, which have over the centuries produced a rich architecture that can equal that of Egypt or Greece but have also developed a conception of space that will not fit into Giedion's neat formulation. For example, that a sense of interiority existed in India is borne out by the earliest rock cut temples dating back to the fourth century BC. True, it is not articulated and written about in theoretical terms as much as the Western heritage, but by the mid-twentieth century, when Giedion's book came out, several studies were available[4] showing that different civilizations may have developed their own conception of space. It would be more fruitful to talk about a plurality of space conceptions than a singular and universal one.

Second, the dialectical progression of the three stages, from an ancient beginning to the present and continuing to move toward a supposed unification, hinted at in the last paragraph of the book, itself is a product of intellectual developments in seventeenth-century Europe, which ushered in rationalism and the linear progression of history. The wind of modernity that blew through Europe with a gale force left no intellectual activity untouched. Architecture was no exception. This can be seen in the marked difference between all theoretical writings in architecture from this period and those preceding it. Starting with Lodoli and Laugier in the eighteenth century, Julien Guadet and Auguste Choisy in the nineteenth and finally in the twentieth century J.M. Richards and H.-R. Hitchcock, all studies have been aimed at interpreting historical architecture of the past in order to build a rational theory which informed much of the modern movement. Giedion too belongs to this group of historians who seek to interpret the past through the lenses of the ideas, values and experiences of the present. This is a departure from the earlier historical studies of Vitruvius, Palladio or Alberti, whose theories were limited to codification or sublimation of past experiences or prevailing practices to explain the intricacies of the art and guide its practitioners. Interpretation, on the other hand, is an ideologically motivated enterprise prone to "foregrounding" only those events of the past that will support the present, relegating others as insignificant. This has not only led Giedion to ignore other civilizations but also to overlook even some aspects of Egyptian architecture which did not support his conclusions, as we shall see below.

For his theoretical research on space Giedion has relied on three European scholars: Alois Riegl of Austria, Heinrich Wolfflin of Switzerland and August Schmarsow of Germany. Riegl, who traced the formation of space from the pyramids to the early Christian period, also propounded the notion of artistic volition—*Kunstwollen*—"which asserts itself in conflict with the requirements of custom, material goods and technical skills,"[5] a concept completely alien to classical Europe but very much in operation during fin-de-siècle Vienna. Riegl also assumed a fixed relationship between the observer and the space as in a perspectival representation. Giedion himself notes that in Riegl's scheme, "The ideal observer is . . . nailed to a fixed viewpoint, both for interior and exterior space" (p. 501). This separation between the observer and the space, between the subject and the object, between the mind and the body was contained within the notion of Euclidian space which was not only antithetical to the earlier sense of perceptual space but which could also emerge only by negating it.

Both Wolfflin, an authority on Renaissance and a disciple of Jacob Burckhardt, and Schmarsow helped establish space as an absolute entity, independent of human experience, and the formation of space—*Raumbildung*—as a fundamental determinant of architecture as art. But these were not the only scholars expounding on the ideas of space. For example, Edmund Husserl (1859–1938), and his close associate and disciple Martin Heidegger (1889–1976) had already questioned the positivist orientation of the science and philosophy of their day, proposing that experience is the source of all knowledge. However, it is clear that the intellectual compass which Giedion accepted did not point him toward these alternative narratives. The magnetic pull of rationalism was indeed overwhelming. Still, it is unfortunate that by not drawing upon these alternative ideas Giedion has missed out on crucial clues that might have enriched his own work. It is possible to construct a different narrative of the Egyptian conception of space, as we shall see below. At the same time, not one, singular and universal narrative but a plurality of narratives of space conception may be available. Even if you consider Egypt, together with Sumer, as the fountainhead of the architectural ideas of the Western hemisphere, a parallel stream, emanating from the Indian sub-continent, offers a critical "other" that can only enrich our understanding of architecture.[6] We shall examine this in the next chapter but here let us investigate below what an alternative space conception might have been in the ancient civilizations of Egypt, one that will not fit into Giedion's neat narrative.

One of the more interesting images of the pyramids in the Lepsius series of 1842 is an imaginary aerial view of the pyramids at Giza (Figure 6.1). What is interesting about this image is that it demonstrates, as Giedion rightly observes, the essential "unity between the pyramid, sky and the limitless desert" (p. 505). The funerary purpose of the pyramids and the evolution of their geometric form have been studied in considerable detail. Their symbolic meaning as the seat of the god-king in his afterlife has also been explored. With pure geometrical triangular surfaces which were originally highly polished, possibly reflecting the movement of clouds in the sky and in the process dematerializing their massive presence, their visual power has been a source of considerable poetic imagination. But their role in the development of the spatial conception has not been properly elaborated.

In order to understand this we have to imagine, for a moment, the desert, as shown in Figure 6.1, without the pyramid. Ancient Egyptians must have faced this vast and limitless space devoid of anything to help them locate or orient themselves. The moment we put back the pyramid in the drawing we realize that, in addition to its funerary and symbolic functions, the pyramid was the most appropriate and effective means for humans to come to terms with the space of the desert. With an imaginary vertical line, originating from the center of the square base and passing through the apex to meet the sky, humans have unmistakably altered an otherwise inhospitable and hostile space by identifying one singular place that they can call their own. However, pyramids cannot be

Figure 6.1
Aerial view of the pyramids at Giza from the Lapsius series. Karl Richard Lepsius, 1849–1959.

seen simply as objects in space claiming a place for humans in the vast empty space. This sublime simplicity of geometry and abstract form, as we see today, conceals a non-objective sense of space with which humans become one with eternity. This did not come about in one singular attempt. A long period of experimentation preceded in which a number of formal alternatives, such as stepped and bent pyramids were tried out before the so-called true pyramid, with four equal isosceles triangles meeting at an apex, was arrived at. At that moment the structure transcended its original funerary purpose and became the embodiment of the collective sense of the cosmic reality. And what was that reality? It was a reality as experienced by humans with their feet planted firmly on the ground and not as represented in Lepsius's aerial view. And besides, today we are so conditioned to see the pyramid as it is today, with its rough exterior surfaces, that we do not realize that the surfaces were indeed highly polished white limestone. While the abstract form and its pure mathematics provided the counterpoint to nature, the highly polished limestone surfaces of the triangles, seen against the equally hot white desert sky, must have challenged the very materiality of the massive form at the same time. Rarely have humans achieved such ambiguity and mystery in dealing with perceptual space. The size of pyramids and their abstract geometric forms speak not only of their symbolic purpose but also of a sense of space in which nothing smaller in size or less abstract in design would have sufficed. To apply the Aristotelian category of continuous quantity, the space itself has "gathered" into a solid form sharing its simple boundaries.

This last point needs to be explored in some detail. I believe we have missed a very important aspect of Egyptian architecture in general and especially their conception of space by thinking that pyramids have always been as we see them today: solid masses of abstract geometry against the vast empty space of the desert. Several Egyptologists[7] have noted that originally the triangular surfaces on all four sides were finished with highly polished limestone. This raises an interesting possibility about the perceptual qualities of pyramids: what if they were never meant to be perceived as solid mass in contrast and possibly in confrontation with the space around them? This binary of space–solid breaks down if the polished white surfaces merged with the hot white sky while reflecting the sunlight. For in this way all the references to earthly realities are negated and the mass is effectively dematerialized. The mass, and its earthly presence has been transformed into an illusion which you see and yet do not "see." The coagulation of space into a mass, to which the Aristotelian category of continuous quantity refers, has been elevated to a sublime spiritual experience merging the spirit of the Pharaoh with eternity.

This captures our basic or fundamental topological and intuitive views regarding space in which space, objects and the observer, as another bodily object, are all integral parts of the same multi-dimensional matrix. The movement of one—a cloud in the sky or the observer with their feet on the ground—will alter the whole. This view was prevalent at the time the map of Rome by *Fra Paolino the Minorite*, was drawn in the fourteenth century (Figure 6.2). If we take a closer look at this map we realize that what has been represented is not what Rome is but what Rome *felt* like as the cartographer bodily moved around, on his feet, from place to place. He drew hills and buildings as he faced them and had to turn around to face other hills and buildings. The cartographer always remained earthbound. He had to bodily move around and at any given time could take in only a partial image of the world around him. The idea of representing the world by imagining oneself bodily separated, as in the mind-body duality, had not yet been developed. What the map presents is the image of an experienced phenomenon and not an abstract idea of the world. This was replaced by the Euclidean *metrical*, or distant, view of space, that eventually was to emerge in the seventeenth century.

The category of void was also alien to this view of space. It was this absence of the idea of void in the objectification process that must explain the great Hypostyle Hall at Karnak, and not any "aversion to interior space" as proposed by Giedion.[8] Not only does the duality of space (void) and solid, as we saw above, but also that of interior and exterior and of the subject and object have no place in the worldview of the early civilizations. It is unfair to the Egyptians to say that they had an aversion to interior space, for we do see some powerful interior spaces even in the early Pharaohic architecture. What these spaces share with that of the Hypostyle Hall is the dimensional relationship between the materiality of the walls, or the columns, and the gaps in between them.

The central colonnade of the Hypostyle Hall was clearly meant for the king's procession through to the temple. But there are no records to establish a clear purpose for the two densely columned flanks on each side of the central colonnade (Figure 6.3). This lack of recorded evidence has led to conjectures that the Egyptians were averse to interior space. Technical determinism, on the other hand, has concluded that an inability to span large areas has resulted in the density of the columns. Neither of these two interpretations throw much light on the likely use of these places, although Giedion does state the obvious that it was "not a gathering place for a congregation of the devout" but then immediately contradicts himself by saying, rather definitively, that "ritual functions were performed and oracles delivered. Pronouncements of the deity were received here."[9] Such speculations do not quite match the peculiar spatial qualities of these dark and dense spaces and that is a serious infirmity in an otherwise

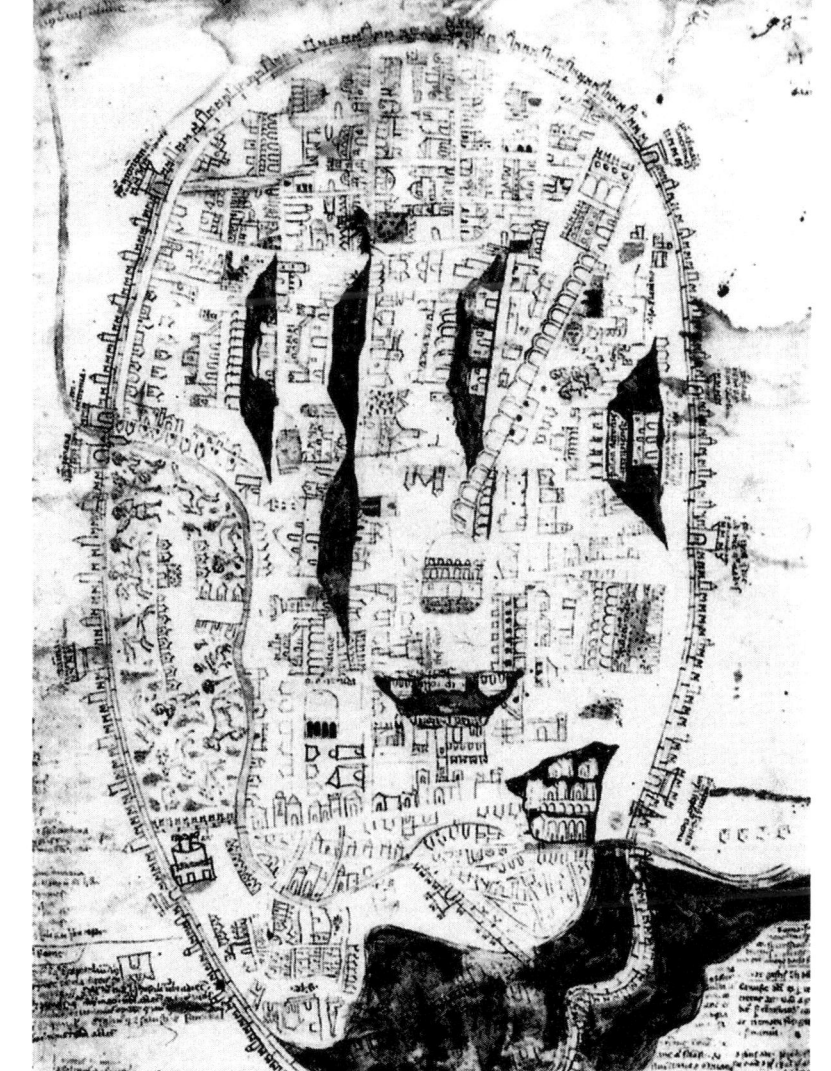

Figure 6.2
**Plan of Rome
in fourteenth-
century codex
by Fra Paolino
the Minorite,
1346.**

rigorous analysis. If one is averse to the interior space and does not know how to span a large space, why make these in the first place? Immense amounts of effort and energy were spent in building these two "halls." We may never know for sure the actual occupational purpose of these places, but still both these conjectures are off the mark for two reasons other than the fact that they do not answer the question of the purpose of these spaces.

Figure 6.3
**Sectional
perspective
rendering of the
Hypostyle Hall,
Karnak, Egypt.
Georges Perrot
and Charles
Chipiez, 1882.**

First, both these interpretations are based on spatial or technical reasoning that emerged several centuries later and is retrospectively applied here and may not be appropriate to the civilization that existed during the Nineteenth Dynasty (1350–1150 BC). The polar categories of interior/exterior spaces, or solids and voids, entered human consciousness only after the construction of large vaulted spaces by the Romans, which was later than 600 BC (the Cloaca Maxima sewer in Rome). This represents a much later stage of the objectification process in which intuition was gradually replaced by observation, which involves a critical "distance" between the world and the observer. In the intuitive and topological sense of space of the Egyptians, such a distance is absent; in fact the observer is part of the space itself, woven with it as in a three-dimensional mesh.

Second, vaulting as a technique was indeed known to the Egyptians. The earliest barrel vaults in Egypt are thought to be those in the granaries at Ramesseum built by Ramesses II, who also built the hypostyle at Karnak. So, the lack of technical knowhow for spanning large distances may not be the reason for the density of columns.

Again, we will have to transport ourselves back in time to the Nineteenth Dynasty in order to look for a probable occupational purpose of these spaces and to better understand their nature. Two characteristics of these spaces are unquestionable; unlike the central aisle, which is lit by the clearstory openings, the columned halls are dark spaces illuminated by an occasional small circular opening in the roof slab throwing a beam of light straight down and whatever little light is reflected off other surfaces (Figure 6.4). In addition, the massive columns are not merely dead masses supporting the roof; they have active surfaces covered almost fully by hieroglyphics and meant to be approached closely for reading. This can be done only by each person carrying their own source of light, an oil lamp or a torch, in their hand. The extent of the glow of light, falling on various columns, will constitute the extent of their spatial "enclosure." This is like being in a dark cave: Egyptians had created caves in the middle of the desert, unmistakable evidence of an intuitive sense of interiority.

Figure 6.4
**Small opening
in the roof slab
bringing light
on the floor.
Hypostyle Hall,
Karnak, Egypt.**

Figure 6.5
**Hieroglyphics
on the column
surfaces.
Hypostyle Hall,
Karnak, Egypt.**

As the devotee, or several devotees, moves about reading the sacred script, each will carry their own spatial enclosure with them, with themself being in the center. Each one is inseparably woven in the mesh of this personal, multi-dimensional space and there are as many spaces as there are devotees. The entire space is thus in dynamic motion and is available to each person only in fragments; never as a whole and at once. Each one ends up constructing a picture of reality which is unique to them. There is no distance from where you can look in and contemplate the whole. The sense of wholeness comes from being one with this reality. This is a conceptual antithesis of the space of which Giedion speaks.

By selectively interpreting the past to validate the present, modern historiography has constructed a one-dimensional modernity. The notion of geometric space, existing independent of human consciousness and experience is one of the pillars of this edifice. The other is the Hegelian view of history, which seeks to arrange events in a linear and logical sequence. But this modernity, so constructed, is devoid of depth because of its inability to incorporate plurality of worldviews in defining its self-identity. We must attend to this infirmity if modernity is to mean anything.

Notes

1 S. Giedion, *Space, Time and Architecture* (Cambridge: Harvard University Press, 1962).
2 S. Giedion, *The Eternal Present: The Beginnings of Architecture* (New York: Bollingen Series, 1964).
3 S. Giedion, *The Eternal Present*, 2.
4 Jacqueline Tyrwhitt, "The Moving Eye." In *Explorations in Communication*, ed. Edmund Carpenter and Marshall McLuhan (Boston: Beacon Press, 1960), 90–95. Interestingly, Tyrwhitt also helped in the preparation of Giedion's second book. Another scholar who wrote extensively on space in India was Stella Kramrisch, then at the Philadelphia Museum.
5 As quoted in S. Giedion, *The Eternal Present*, 500.
6 I have extensively dwelt on the Indian conception of space in my previous two books, *Rethinking Modernity* (2011) and *Embodied Vision* (2014). Readers may refer to these.
7 Michel Vallogia (University of Geneva); Joanne Rowlands (University of Oxford); Zahi Hawass (Secretary General, Supreme Council of Antiquities, Egypt).
8 S. Giedion, *The Eternal Present*, 509.
9 Ibid., 387.

Chapter 7

Architecture as Co-Making

Conventionally we consider architecture and architectural space as an objective entity, contemplated by us as something independent of our body, and described through the Euclidian coordinates of x, y and z. This is also often referred to as cognitive space or geometric space. We are so conditioned by this notion of space that we think it has always been so for ever and do not admit of any other way of thinking about architectural space.

In reality, though, this is a legacy of the seventeenth-century scientific revolution which determined that only the objective truth, verifiable by empirical evidence, can be real. However, the conception of space that architecture deals with is quite complex. Great architecture throughout history has always transcended our cognitive capacities and has touched us in a deep and spiritual way. To build an architectural space conception primarily around our cognitive and rational faculties alone is to miss out on the experiential and spiritual aspects of architecture. We will have to enlarge our conception of space to incorporate in it those qualities and human experiences so far left out.

Architecture deals with three simultaneous notions of space: (1) cognitive space, (2) perceptual space and (3) mythical space. Unlike cognitive space, which is objective and independent of the human body and engages our faculty of reason, both perceptual space and mythical space are contingent upon bodily presence and the active participation of the occupier/user of the space. In that sense, architectural space is always co-made by the physicality of the architectural object on the one hand and the occupier/user on the other. In other words, our very occupation of space entails an active dialog, a conversation, between our bodily movement within the space and the objective conditions of architecture.

For a demonstration of the perceptual/existential qualities, we will have to devise a method that relies more on natural *seeing*, rather than abstract *viewing*, and allow our bodies, standing on our two feet, to be encompassed and enveloped by the elements of the building. The images we gather will naturally be a series of partial images, limited by the scope of our perceptual capacities and not an overall grand image of the whole at a time. We shall replace the "mind's eye view" with a view offered by "eyes of the skin,"[1] in the words of *Juhani Pallasmaa*. As we walk through the building, it does not unfold but *enfolds* us. The spaces acquire characteristics which are contingent upon our presence within them; they lose independent meanings. Architecture is "co-made" by the building and the occupier/observer. The quality of light shapes our perception to a large extent. It determines the sense of confinement and release. The materiality of the walls, with their rough texture, makes us acutely aware of the distance between them and our shoulders. In fact, being acutely aware of our physical being is one of the interesting corollaries of such an experience. Unlike a Renaissance painting, where the vanishing point of a scene is within and on the other side of the picture plane, we carry the vanishing point in our own selves all the time as we move. This blurs the distinction between the subject and the object.[2]

Prior to the scientific revolution, our conception of space had been centered on our bodies. We referred to space always in reference to our own bodies and their position. The relations of "here," "there," "in front," "behind," "to my right," "to my left," "above," "below" and so on are all spatial relations. But they are not just given to us along with our simple sensations. They are highly complex, thoroughly mediated products of empirical judgment. They are anchored and referenced to our bodies and specific to each of us. For example, if you are standing on my left, the same cannot be said if the reference changes from me to you; I am on your right. Similarly, when we attribute size, position and distance to things in space, we are not expressing simple sensations but are situating the sensory data in relation to our own self; the distances are to be measured not in abstract units of feet or meters but by the number of paces something is away from our body standing on its two feet on the ground. The space stretches away in all directions with our body as the center. This calls for an act of pure judgment. Let us call this the perceptual space. Interestingly, this had been the standard conception of space accepted universally until the sixteenth century.

An alternative idea of space emerged around the beginning of the seventeenth century in Europe precisely because of the changes brought about in the ways humans can perceive the world around them. I refer to Galileo's invention of the telescope, which shattered the certainty of the geocentric worldview, founded on the basis of what was perceived by our senses to be true. What followed this seemingly innocuous event was no less than a revolution. For what Galileo did, and what no one had done before, was to use the telescope in such a way that the secrets of the universe were delivered within the grasp of an earthbound creature and its body-bound senses. What had seemed forever beyond reach, at best open to the uncertainties of speculation and imagination was now empirically available. For example, even in ancient times the Greek mathematician, physicist, engineer, inventor and astronomer Archimedes of Syracuse (c. 287 BC to c. 212 BC) is supposed to have claimed that given a place to stand on in space and a big enough lever he could move the earth. And not many years before Galileo, the great boldness of mathematically trained Copernicus's imagination had lifted him from the earth and enabled him to look down upon it as though he were an inhabitant of one of the planets in outer space. So long as these efforts remained in the realm of imagination, the establishment—and that included the powerful Church—had no problem and tolerated them. Galileo's telescope, however, constituted an event involving an instrument liberating humans from their body-bound senses. What he found out was not what people had believed to be true all this time. It established that the senses are not reliable and the apparent is not real. And that the "truth" will have to be arrived at by observation and the rigorous application of the human intellect with the help of instruments. It led to the development of modern science and mathematics, including geometry. It gave birth to an idea of space that can be termed the "space of pure cognition" as opposed to the "space of sense perception." Its language of description was pure geometry as laid down in 300 BC by Euclid the Greek mathematician of Alexandria. It is generally referred to as Euclidian space.

What are the attributes of Euclidian space? How do we distinguish it from the perceptual space? Ernst Cassirer[3] lists three basic attributes of Euclidian space: continuity, infinity and homogeneity. That is a good place to start. But then immediately we realize that all these qualities answer to one overarching master attribute: they are all independent and outside the bodily experience of humans. Therein lies the source of the antithetical relationship between the two conceptions of space: all these qualities can never be attributed to the visual and tactile space of perception. The very fact that our faculties of perception—visual, tactile, olfactory and so on, all residing in our bodies—are confined within a certain spatial limit makes the concept of infinity alien to the space of perception; we can perceive only that which is available to our senses.

Similarly, homogeneity or uniformity can never be attributed to perception. Imagine a simple geometric cube made up of eight vertices, *a, b, c, d, e, f, g* and *h* joined together by twelve lines which inscribe a space, the most elementary representation of the Euclidian space (Figure 7.1). The basis of the homogeneity of this space is that all the vertices which are joined in it determine only their position in relation to each other and have no independent meaning of their own outside of these relations. As Cassirer puts it:

> Because fundamentally these points are devoid of all content, because they have become mere expressions of ideal relations, they can raise no question of a diversity of content. Their homogeneity signifies nothing other than this similarity of structure, grounded in their common logical function, their common ideal purpose and meaning.[4]

For example, the meanings of the vertices can be expressed thus: assuming that *a* is zero, then *b* is one meter on the *x* axis, *d* is one meter on the *y* axis and *e* is one meter on the *z* axis, and so on. Thus if there is any meaning/content which can be attributed to these vertices, it is exhausted in such description of their relations vis-à-vis each other. None of them have independent meaning and therefore no question of diversity. The cube can be replicated on all six sides potentially up to infinity, and it is outside our body and the realm of its experiences. It is purely cognitive and we think about it the way Archimedes thought about the earth.

Mythical space can be located somewhere between the perceptual space and the cognitive space and shares some attributes with each of them. Like the space of perception, it requires our bodily occupation of the space and at the same time it is also defined by a series of vertices like the cognitive space, though these vertices are always loaded with meaning, unlike the vertices of the cube.

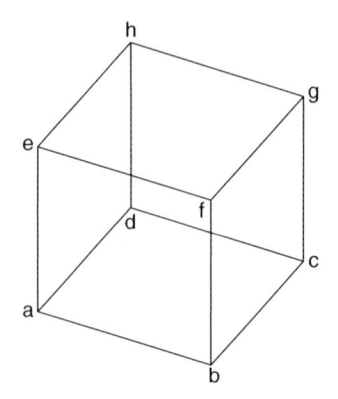

Figure 7.1
Cube, simple representation of geometric space.

The city of Bhaktapur in Nepal is a good example of this (Figure 7.2). The sacred space of the city is inscribed by eight shrines/temples (vertices) dedicated to eight mother goddesses, *Astamatrikas*. These form the path of circumambulation which a devotee bodily traverses and in the process inscribes *a* space. This is not a space of abstract geometry, to be contemplated through cerebral distance, but rather a space to be bodily engaged and co-made by the physicality of the shrines' location in geographical terrain, the meanings and the myth embedded in each shrine/temple and the re-enactment of the composite myth of *Astamatrikas* by the devotees walking with their feet firmly on the ground. It is finite and grounded at a specific location on earth and cannot be replicated elsewhere. Each vertex (shrine) is distinct from the other both in terms of its specific location and also the diversity of stories it carries. Each one embodies a meaning distinct from the others.

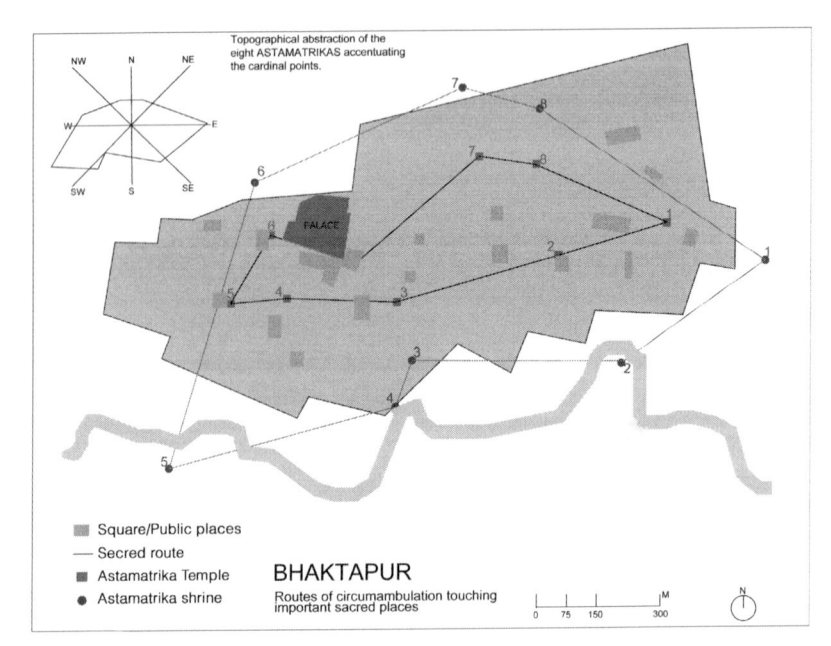

Figure 7.2
Space inscribed by circumambulation by devotees. Bhaktapur, Nepal.

Thus Cassirer's three basic attributes of Euclidian space—continuity, infinity and homogeneity—do not apply here. And yet the city's comprehension requires a cerebral engagement and not the sensorial "eyes of the skin" as would be the case for a purely perceptual space. This space, in its mythical form, is available only to those steeped in the legends and mythologies of the place, for its co-making requires an active conversation between the physical and the mythical, between the objective entity of architectural form and the human presence. It is made and re-made every time the stories are re-enacted by the devotees. The space is comprehended not so much by seeing it from a distance but by travers- ing its edges from shrine to shrine and completing the circumambulation.

The Brihadeshwara temple complex at Tanjavur in south India is a large con- glomeration of various smaller shrines and other supporting structures around the main temple (Figure 7.3). While the main temple in the center displays geometric order, the platforms, as well as the steps leading up to them are not on any axis. The arrangement of other shrines seems haphazard, informal and incremental, conceived over a period of time, which it may have been. At first glance, it does not seem rigorous enough. But this would be an interpretation founded on our present rational/visual criteria. In order to understand it we will have to transpose ourselves in time to when it was built in the year AD 1010.

Brihadeshwara is the birth place of one of the many classical Indian dance forms, *Bharatnatyam*. Devotees would come here not only to offer prayers but also to dance; often the offering itself took the form of a dance whereby the dancer became an integral part of the space re-enacting the myths connected with the lords Shiva, Kartikeya or Ganesha, and the *Ashta-dikpaalakas* (eight guardians of the directions, Indra, Agni, Yama, Nirṛti, Varuṇa, Vāyu, Kubera, and Īśāna)—each of whom was originally represented by a life-sized statue, approximately 6 feet tall, enshrined in a separate temple located in the respective direction. The pos- sible movement of the dancer, which begins at the main *Gopuram*, traverses the

Figure 7.3
Brihadeshwara
temple.
Tanjavur, India,
AD **1010.**

entire space in a complex, non-linear fashion, and ends on the platform in front of the main shrine (Figure 7.4), revealing that the spatial disposition of the various elements has something to do with myths and their re-enactment (Figure 7.5). If the lines connecting the various shrines at Bhaktapur circumscribe and thus define the sacred space within this "enclosure," at Brihadeshwara this space is far more complex. It is not linear and folds upon itself.

The *Brihadeshwara* temple is a house for god containing many mansions to enshrine the god's various manifestations. The interrelationship with each of these parts is established by the dancer/devotee moving within the space and re-enacting the myth. He is an integral part of making of this space. The space of *Brihadeshwara*, a space created in motion, transcends the fundamental dichotomy of subject and object, which is the essence of Cartesian space. The observer, in such an empirical, Cartesian space, is not a participant in the making of the space; they are an outsider and the objective reality is outside them.

In *Brihadeshwara* this dichotomy is overcome. The observer is very much a part of the space. The space is made only on that condition. When the observer becomes one with the space of the temple, it no longer remains for them a symbol of the cosmos, it becomes the cosmos. Each observer is on their own journey. Therefore there may be as many spaces as many observers, as many dancers.[5]

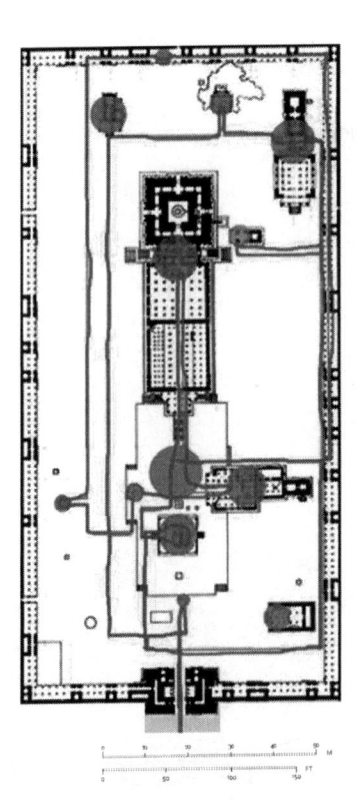

Figure 7.4
Plan of Brihadeshwara. A devotee traverses the entire space in the ritual movement connecting various sacred shrines.

Figure 7.5
**Interpretive
reconstruction
showing the
interaction
between the
dancer and the
space.**

All over the world, and in every society throughout history, people have sought to construct stories and myths that make sense of the diversity of their world. The impulse is both romantic and practical and every narrative is a simplification of individual events that are stitched together to constitute it. Architecture thus becomes the "totem pole" of the culture for projecting these narratives through visual form. However, such a transformation is not limited to pre-rational examples such as Bhaktapur or Brihadeshwara, where the "reading" of space is contingent upon the movement of the dancer/devotee and their interaction with the objective architecture of the temple. Although communication through symbolic forms, and the resultant conversation between architecture and the human participants, was far more prevalent in pre-rational societies, more recent examples are also available and indicate that architecture has always been involved in iconic communication. In our own so-called high-rational societies one still comes across events when dynamic architectural spaces have been created by engaging us in a conversation with the new icons of our own era.

I refer to the US pavilion at the Montreal World's Fair of 1967, designed by Buckminster Fuller and Cambridge Seven Associates (Figure 7.6). The building was a simple geodesic dome containing a series of platforms, at various levels, connected by escalators. The entire volume of this spherical space was filled with a series of objects or images which represented the prevalent "myth" of the United States in the mid-twentieth century (Figure 7.7). This was the time when the US had captured the imagination of the world with both its soft power, that is, Hollywood, Pop Art, and so on, as well as the technological achievement of conquering outer space. Thus we see icons such as Marlon Brando, Marlene Dietrich, the ubiquitous urban yellow cab and Andy Warhol as well as the lunar landing craft and space ship (Figures 7.8 and 7.9). The space is made and remade for each visitor by their movement through the space and the relationship (conversation) they may establish with these icons—of familiarity, pride, joy, awe or envy. In this sense, their movement through this space is not much different from that of the dancer devotee at the Brihadeshwara temple. The images collectively represented the spirit of United States at that time and to that extent the experience of them was spiritual. It was independent from the spherical volume contained by the dome; in fact both acted as counterpoints for each other.

Figure 7.6
**US pavilion
at Expo 67.
R. Buckminster
Fuller and
Cambridge
Seven
Associates,
Montreal,
Canada, 1967.**

Figure 7.7
**Interior of the
US pavilion,
Cambridge
Seven
Associates,
Montreal,
Canada, 1967.**

Figure 7.8
Interior of the US pavilion, Cambridge Seven Associates, Montreal, Canada, 1967.

Figure 7.9
Interior of the US pavilion, Cambridge Seven Associates, Montreal, Canada, 1967.

This space presupposes the presence of human visitors; in fact it loses all meaning in the absence of human presence, for each of these images and icons embody meanings that are encrypted in the cultural ethos and can be revealed only through an active engagement of people in space. The icon/image/object, space and the moving observer assume uniformity as if they are all made of the same substance, like a three-dimensional mesh assuming various forms but connecting all. The movement of the observer constantly alters the relationship between the icon/image and the observer. If the "dance" of the moving observer is a motion in space, architecture is thus space in motion.

The iconography may differ between Bhaktapur, Brihadeshwara and the US pavilion at Montreal but the space is similar. In all cases the observer is an integral part of the phenomena to be observed. The distinction between the "subject" and the "object" is overcome. Architecture is co-made by the physicality of the built form and the human presence. This offers us a tentative sketch of a possible alternative conception of space for architecture. Theory is sublimation of experience. Let us accept that architectural experiences throughout history and in all parts of the world have always dealt with a far more complex space than what we have theorized so far.

Notes

1 Juhani Pallasmaa, *The Eyes of the Skin* (London: John Wiley & Sons, 2005).
2 Stella Kramrisch, *A Survey of Painting in the Deccan* (New Delhi: Oriental Reprint, 1983), 3–8.
3 Ernst Cassirer, *The Philosophy of Symbolic Forms*, vol. 2 (New Haven: Yale University Press, 1968), 83.
4 Ernst Cassirer. Ibid., 84.
5 Vrinda Pant, "Architecture and Dance" (undergraduate dissertation, School of Architecture, CEPT University, 1999).

Chapter 8

Vaastu and the Enfolding Order

Recently someone advanced a suggestion in an English daily newspaper that our Parliament House in Delhi should be checked against the norms and strictures of the ancient practice of *Vaastu* as, according to him, its entrance is not properly aligned and that is the reason why we experience turbulent political times now. He also proposed concrete alterations, including shifting the entrance from its present location, to improve the health of our polity and by extension that of the nation.

I have no doubt that the gentleman was genuinely concerned and meant well. However, the solution suggested seems too good to be true. For if the health of a human institution, with 500-plus members with their own constituencies, geographically located in all corners of the country, with differing human, social, economic and political compulsions, can be so easily altered then the world could be a much better, though personally I think a far less interesting, place to be. Besides, the fact that the same Parliament house, with the same entrance, has functioned reasonably well in the first few decades of this republic makes me wonder if we are investing architecture with too much temporal power.

This is a recent phenomenon. True, ancient India has had a wealth of wisdom in the matters of construction of human habitat and cities. At last count there are more than 50 ancient titles, some dating back to the first millennium, collectively referred to as *Vaastu Shastra* that have existed as part of our Vedic and Upanishadic heritage for centuries. However, it is during the last few decades that *Vaastu Shastra* has captured the interest of many as something that may offer solutions to many of our present-day problems and so, they say, should be revived. Its present popularity may be due to the campaign for its revival in the 1980s by the late Mr. Vaidyanatha Ganapati Sthapati, then Principal of the Government College of Architecture and Sculpture, University of Madras. He belonged to the family of traditional *sthapatis* (temple architects) in Tamil Nadu and took upon himself the task to revive the traditional knowledge system. However, in its present form it is mostly seen as a series of dos and don'ts, a set of desired practices, for constructing our earthly habitation. It is often seen as claiming causal connection between the design of our buildings and events in the temporal life of the owner/occupant. Opinions vary about the beneficent, or otherwise, effects of these practices. The rationalists among us dismiss it as a lot of "hocus pocus" without any scientific basis, while the believers stand by it firmly and claim it to be "scientific" in all its contemporary connotations. There is a wide range in between occupied by most of us wherein we either follow it or not depending upon the level of our insecurities; if we are not sure why our business is not doing well, we might as well seek some advice and realign our office layout and hope that it may propitiate the cosmic forces in our favor. Most contemporary practicing architects, me included, whose training has been firmly rooted in the rationalist modern thinking, find it difficult to resist if a client insists and give in to a compromise or refuse a commission (though this rarely happens).

I must admit that I have not done a detailed and definitive study of the ancient scriptures. My attempts to find a teacher who can lead me through the ideas and practices contained therein (mostly written in *Sanskrit*), without presenting it as a dogma, have not been very successful. However, after going through several English translations (there are various versions by different authors, both ancient and modern), I feel that our ancestors have left a well of wisdom which we ignore only at our own peril. But first it is essential that we understand the nature of the work and put it in the global context of human knowledge systems.

Vaastu Shastra is a knowledge system, a part of the tradition which evolved during Vedic times (1500–500 BC) and has come down to us first through oral tradition and then, after the first millennium, through literary compilations. Of all the existing texts, two are most comprehensive: one, originating in south India and known as *Mayamatam*, dates from between the ninth and twelfth centuries; the other, known as *Manasara*, dates from between the fifth and seventh centuries and is also not attributed to a single author but is a compilation of eleven different manuscripts whose authorship is varied and obscure.

These are both supposed to be sets of rules that govern the practice of architecture. In that sense, *Vaastu Shastra* can be said to be the sublimation of a culture's experiences and codification of the artisanal practices prevalent during Vedic times. The present uneasiness among the rationalists stems from the fact that today it is placed above and beyond the practical craft of building, as a sort of eternal divine wisdom preexisting humans. Is *Vaastu* a divine theory that may guide the practice of architecture? Is it "scientific" in a contemporary sense? It is important to ask these questions since that seems to be the popular perception among believers. A theory, as in the case of scientific theories, is supposed to explain the principles underlying a phenomenon and would be equally applicable to all phenomena with similar characteristics with minimum number of exceptions. In that case, Einstein's theory of relativity can be called a theory as it explains the cosmic architecture with remarkable consistency and although quantum mechanics and String theory are posing serious challenges to its primacy, it is likely to remain in this position for some time. Similarly, Newton's laws of optics and the laws of gravity are theoretical postulates in the same category. All such theories are based on observations or practices, which when generalized lead to an explanation of similar phenomena and, beyond that, of how the world around us works.

This tells us about three characteristics of all theoretical postulates: (1) During its currency, a theory is singular and unchallenged in its own area of concern. This singularity is independent of cultural or geographic variations and should satisfy universal applications. In other words, there cannot be two separate theories of gravitation at the same time. (2) Theories follow, and are based on, observations and practices. They do explain the "divine" order, if you want to call it that, but are certainly not divine edicts handed down to us from beyond. They are all human constructs subject to reconstruction when new observations and practices so require. In short, practices precede and engender theory, and not the other way round. (3) A theory should be able to predict causality. In other words, if a theory postulates that action A causes reaction B, then we should be able to predict that in all circumstances action A will cause reaction B. Such certainty is a characteristic of scientific theory.

Architecture is a vocational activity as well as a discipline, as pure science or philosophy would be disciplines. For a vocation, the basis of a theoretical construct would be practice while it would be empirical observations or speculation for a discipline, which results in ideas that inform the practices from time to time. Thus there is a dialectical relationship between theory and practice. To understand the origin of theoretical formulation in a vocational activity we must look at the earliest craft practices of our forefathers. I put forward the following as a possible scenario.

As early humans began to settle down in one place to pursue agriculture, their initial attempts to build shelters were direct and simple responses to the forces of nature they encountered with whatever materials were available to them. These activities went on for a long time, probably for centuries. During this time the practices were repeated again and again with some variations and as time passed, these repetitions and observations must have provided judgments about the soundness of some solutions over the others. Some ways of laying out a house seemed to be better and more satisfying than others. Some ways of building a roof may have seemed better than others.

Over centuries some of these chosen building solutions acquired the natural authority of truth. They carried in them a consensus and the accumulated wisdom of the entire community. They transcended the origin of a particular solution (such as a gable or porch) and acquired the status of universal laws. While looking at them everyone recognized in them the cumulative knowledge, wisdom and experience of their community and these were passed on from one generation to the next as collective memories ("*smruti*" or "remembrance") of desirable practices. It was much later, when several such desirable practices were evolved in response to the needs of building not only houses but also palaces, temples, monasteries, even prisons and so on that there may have been an attempt to codify them so that they become accessible to everyone.

This process of documentation and codification must have been undertaken essentially by scholars and pundits and not by the craftsmen who actually executed the work. Thus a degree of simplification, generalization and abstraction is inevitable. Such codifications, by their very nature, have to be free of any specific contextual references. For example, it may be said that while laying out a town, the streets shall be straight and intersect each other at right angles. However, the builders and craftsmen, while laying a town, may encounter a hill or a pond and may turn the street around to avoid destroying it. In their mind the street would still be "straight." The pundits may not have specified all such exceptions but somewhere they would have elaborated on humankind's relationship with nature to sanctify the variation and would approve.

This process of codification goes beyond simply providing rules for future human actions, it also indicates a civilization's worldview, encompassing its ideas about the nature of humans, of nature, the relationship between humans and nature and between individual humans; in other words, an all-encompassing set of beliefs that distinguishes one civilization from others. In India, the texts I mentioned above should be read as a part of the entire Vedic wisdom, which presents a distinct worldview. And that is precisely the reason why such codification as theoretical works can never be universally singular. Every civilization around the world will have its own worldview and that would lead to a plurality of such works. For example, the first-century Roman architect Vitruvius's work *The Ten Books on Architecture* was a similar codification of the accumulated experience of centuries of work in Mesopotamia, Egypt and Greece.

It is important to dwell a bit more on Vitruvius's work because I find it to be a good foil against which the broad contours of the Vedic thoughts can be understood. In the very first chapter of his treatise, Vitruvius has summarized his work thus: public buildings "must be built with due reference to durability, convenience, and beauty,"[1] implying that architecture can be said to exist when these three conditions are present. This summation of Vitruvius is of interest for two reasons. First, it can be said to be the first truly theoretical formulation in the sense that, beyond mere codification, it provides a structure to the practice of architecture. What Vitruvius has done is a classic example of analysis: reduction of a phenomenon into its component parts and their reconstitution into an intellectual entity—a theoretical postulate. Such a postulate not only explains architecture by laying bare its essential components but also helps us predict that architecture will happen when the conditions specified therein are present; in other words, its causality. What distinguishes Vitruvius, however, is that he practiced what may be referred to as the analytical/logical/rational mode of thinking. Such thinking is the product of a reflecting consciousness. It is in the nature of a reflecting consciousness to reflect upon the objective world around it in an attempt to find and articulate laws which govern it. In other words, the sublimation of reality as it is *revealed* to humans. But this revelation must first be channeled through the human intellect to be a theoretical postulate.

Is *Vaastu* then a theory, like that of Vitruvius, that may guide the practice of architecture? My answer would be a qualified yes and no. I certainly would not like to place it as a divine edict beyond question or possibility of interpretations. At the same time I would also not like to discard it as unscientific and therefore not worthy of a rational and logical mind. Here, we may make a distinction between tradition and orthodoxy. Tradition is a living and continuously evolving process of creation and preserves what continues to remain significant responding to the new situations, while orthodoxy takes over when tradition ceases to be alive. It fossilizes tradition into lifeless structure often presenting it as divine edict. Though interrupted for a thousand years and its natural growth stunted, I want to view *Vaastu* as a tradition that is still alive and which allows growth and development in new directions. But first it must be rescued from orthodoxy.

Seen as such, the Vedic thought, of which *Vaastu* is a product, is no less a product of the same reflecting consciousness. This reflecting consciousness led Western people to the path of a rational, logical, scientific worldview while the Vedic people developed a view of their world that we can term "mythical" or transcendental. The difference stems from the assumed relationship between the reflecting subject and the objective world; the former saw the two as separate and independent from each other, the latter, as we shall see below, found a unity and wholeness.

So we have at least two different worldviews co-existing at the same time. On one hand there is the analytical/rational view, the highest manifestation of which is the form and structure of science, particularly the "exact" science of nature, and on the other hand there is the mythical worldview whose methods and judgments are more transcendental and intuitive but no less products of an intellectual act. We shall look into the differences between them shortly but we can be sure of the one commonality between them: they both are looking for the unity, that something that makes sense of the infinite variety and manifoldness of the sensuous, experiential world within which we find ourselves. This is the primary aim of all human consciousness. The world of our sensuous experience, what we see, hear, touch and taste is so vast and full of variety and diversity that it would be maddening and thoroughly disorienting for humans to be on this planet without evolving an ordering schema which makes sense of it all. Each major civilization has evolved such schemata founded on the values each has held high; in fact they are distinguished from each other by this very difference. Their paths may be different, their modalities for arriving at the truth may be different but their aim is the same.

There is a vast amount of literature in philosophy and psychology regarding the peculiarities and differences between scientific/analytical thought and mythical thought. It is not my intention to dwell elaborately on the intricately nuanced philosophical discourse here. Still, we will have to briefly summarize the relevant ideas to take our present inquiry further, although it must be emphasized at the outset that these are two alternative and equally rational thought systems that cannot be subjected to a hierarchy in which one is deemed superior to the other. Pure analytical thought, which has provided the dominant view of the world since the sixteenth century, has led to the exponential growth in science and technology and brought us to where we are, on the scale of development, but has also come with the attendant problems of environment degradation, unsustainability and the fearful possibility of total annihilation. Still, over the years, it has also conditioned us to assume that it represents the higher level of thought evolution and therefore the preferred way to comprehend the world.

Two consequences follow with regards to analytical thought having acquired the dominant position over the last four centuries. First, the proponents of this scientific/analytical/rational thought relegated mythical thought to a lower level of primitive consciousness and associated it with superstitions and magic unable to stand up to scientific rigor and scrutiny. Second, the revivalists of the mythical consciousness, on the other hand, felt compelled to explain it only through the categories of the former, which was never going to be easy or convincing.[2]

Both analytical thinking and mythical thinking are distinguished from each other by their respective concepts of the *object* (space) and *causality* (time). The two concepts condition each other: the form of the objective thinking determines the form of the causal thinking, and vice versa. It is at this level of the fundamental nature of the two thought systems that we will explore whether the ideas contained in the texts of *Vaastu Shastra* constitute exact analytical scientific thinking or mythical thinking.

Objective thinking is perhaps most evident in the way we represent our spatial relations such as "together," "separate," "side by side," "in front of," "behind," "above," "below" and so on. These relations are highly complex and thoroughly mediated forms of analytical thought requiring judgment. Every object in our external environment is thus differentiated in terms of its position, size and distance, and this can only be grasped and assigned meaning because

> the separate sensory impressions are differently regarded by the judgment and a different *significance* is imputed to them . . . the spatial order of the world of perception thus involves acts of identification, differentiation, comparison and coordination which in their basic form are purely intellectual acts.[3]

This imputation of significance and attributes to objective phenomena is an act aimed at a supreme, universal synthesis resulting in comprehension of the otherwise undifferentiated contents and configurations of perception. But ironically, this *synthesis* toward which analytical thought strives always presupposes a corresponding *analysis* and only on the basis of such analysis can the synthesis be affected. That is to say, the entire jumble of initial experience has to be separated into phenomena (objects) and relationships (ground) first, and only then is its recombination into comprehensible synthetic unity possible. Thus analytical thinking first has to break down the particular contents of experience into their constitutive factors, in order to re-create them genetically. We experience the onset of summer and the arrival of swallows as concurrent, side-by-side phenomena, but when this experience is subjected to the process of analysis and synthesis, we declare that the swallow *does not* make the summer. This is because the world of sense experience is now encompassed in a new order and this new order demands that the elements which stand undifferentiated side by side in immediate perception be gradually distinguished, that what is mere coexisting perception be transposed into an orderly system of cause and effect.

Since the sixteenth century the basic order in modern science has been that of the Cartesian rectilinear grid, modified slightly by the theory of relativity to a curvilinear grid. With this, modern science has had enormous development but the basic order has remained unchanged. This Cartesian order has been highly suitable for the analysis of the world into separate phenomena (e.g., objects, particles, field elements, etc.). But the developments in relativity and quantum theory have shown the Cartesian order as problematic by implying that the actual state of affairs is an unbroken wholeness of the universe which does not lend itself to analysis into independent parts.

This has always been the crisis of analytical thought and it is embedded in the original separation between the reality as the object of reflection and the reflecting consciousness as the subject. But one cannot avoid the question of wholeness and totality in reflecting on and pondering the nature of reality, both in thought and in the object of thought. As the physicist and philosopher David Bohm has so eloquently said:

> The notion that the one who thinks (the ego) is at least in principle completely separate from and independent of the reality that he thinks about is of course firmly embedded in our entire tradition. General experience . . . suggests very strongly that such a division cannot be maintained consistently. But this confronts us with a very difficult challenge: How are we to think coherently of a single, unbroken, flowing actuality of existence as a whole, containing both thought (consciousness) and external reality as we experience it?[4]

Mythical thinking too resides in the realm of pure forms which it regards as thoroughly objective reality (*Brahmaand*). However, unlike analytical thinking, this reality is not subjected to analysis and then re-synthesized into a new order distinguishing between truth and appearances. On the contrary, it is left completely homogeneous and undifferentiated. It seeks to comprehend the totality of existence as an unbroken whole. Mythical thought overcomes the infirmity of subject–object duality by developing a notion of the objective reality (concept of object) and of order, that may be appropriate to a universe of unbroken wholeness. This is the *enfolded* (as opposed to *unfolded*) order in which space (contiguity, proximity, togetherness, apartness, etc.) and time (causality) are no longer the dominant factors determining the relationships of dependence or independence of different elements. In fact if we examine myth, any kind of separation of subject from the object, ideal from the real, distinction between a world of immediate perception and the world of mediate, signification as well as the opposition of "image" and "object" is alien to mythical thinking. Simply put, the image is the object and a swallow *does* make the summer.

This brings us to the concept of causality. In fact the universal category of cause and effect is one of the fundamentals of mythical thinking. There have been a number of legends about the origin of the world or birth of various gods or the beginning of events to suggest that a robust concept of causality existed within mythical thinking. The most interesting characteristic that distinguishes mythical thinking from pure scientific analytical thinking is its proposition that nothing in the world happens at random and every event or phenomenon is connected to a cause, however distant or arbitrary it may seem. Myth proceeds with an intuitive assumption that all occurrences in the universe are for a purpose and that all forces in nature are nothing other than expression of a demonic or divine will.[5]

Consequently, mythical thinking is unable to conceive of an "accident" in the same way as analytical thinking thinks of it as an occurrence which could not be predicted as it cannot be explained in terms of the available categories of space and time. An untimely death, a decline in fortune, the failure of an enterprise or even the breakdown of parliamentary decorum must all be attributed to some cause because in a universe which is an unbroken whole, an enfolded order, everything is contiguous and "anything can *come from* anything, because anything can stand in temporal or spatial contact with anything."[6]

For our scientifically conditioned minds this may seem fantastic, arbitrary, irrational and inferior to the exact science of analytical thinking and we may be tempted to dismiss it without a second thought. But such a conclusion will be premature because the very nature of mythical consciousness demands that we do not reflect upon it from outside but locate ourselves within its unbroken sphere.

But this is precisely what is *not* being done by those seeking to revive *Vaastu Shastra* today. Vedic thought, including *Vaastu*, is the product of mythical consciousness developed on the Indian soil and is a highly sophisticated alternative view of the world. The notion of wholeness is non-negotiable for mythical consciousness. It even refuses to entertain the duality of the reflecting subject, "I" and the object of reflection, the world, by the unambiguous proposition that the universe is non-dual (*Advaita*) and seeks a state of experience (as opposed to reflection) of the infinite (*ananta*) and non-different (*advaita/abheda*), free from the dualistic experience which results from the attempts to conceptualize reality.

This rejection of duality is resolved in the transcendental philosophy of the *Upanishads*. According to this thought, the reflecting consciousness, the self, is distinguished from the not-self, such as the human body, which in reality is part of the external world of forms, and is named *Atman*. The external world (*Brahmaand*), on the other hand, with its infinite variety of manifestations and forms, was also thought to have come from a single source, the world-self, as distinguished from its physical embodiment, the material universe, and needed to be identified. This came to be named *Brahman*. But we encounter an interesting twist here. In a series of lectures he delivered in the 1930s at Mysore University, and referring to *Taittriya Upanishad*, M. Hirianna has this to say:

> The method there was *objective*, for it proceeded by *analyzing* the outer world and not by looking inward as in the line of speculation of which Atman was the goal. In accordance with the general spirit of Indian speculation, several conceptions were evolved here also . . . each more satisfying than the previous one to account for the universe and Brahman was the last of the series of solutions. At some stage in the evolution of thought, the primal source of the universe, viz. Brahman, was identified with its inmost essence, viz. Atman. Thus two independent currents of thought—one resulting from the desire to understand the true nature of man and the other, that of the objective world—became blended and the blending led at once to the discovery of the unity for which there had been such a prolonged search.[7]
>
> (italics mine)

Atman then refers to the reflecting consciousness and *Brahman* the objective world of forms, the object of such reflection. Both spring from the same cosmic energy. With this unity, any distinction between the subject and object, the fundamental categories of analytical thought, disappears.[8]

This comprehensive view of the world permeates, orders and guides all human activities, including the practice of *Vaastu*. And it is within this philosophical context that the various instructions and specifications given in the ancient texts should be interpreted. It is relevant here to refer back to the key concepts of *shruti* and *smruti* mentioned earlier and read them with the notion of "*dharma*," or the code of conduct of an individual. *Shruti*, as we have seen, refers to the eternal ideas or the cosmic laws that govern the universe (*Brahmaand*), with the objective to maintain the cosmic unity and equilibrium. *Smruti*, on the other hand, refers to the rules originating from human activities laying down the best practices for the people at a given place and time and is by its very nature contextual. For *smruti* is always the accumulated knowledge of a people, passed on and added onto from generation to generation, and takes into consideration the spatial, temporal and qualitative (*desha, kala* and *guna*) evolution of the phenomenal world. Thus instructions and specifications based on *smruti* can never be taken as rigid and invariable dogma or a divine edict. They must be interpreted and contextualized and made relevant from time to time. But this interpretation must occur within the context of the eternal laws which always speak about the undifferentiated wholeness, unity and equilibrium of the universe. And it is the *dharma* of an architect to make the right choices in every situation. This scheme contains an element of variability (interpretation) and also of constancy (eternal laws).

The attempts of many of the present day practitioners of *Vaastu*, referred to as "Vaastu Consultants," is directed toward establishing an unequivocal relation between *specific* "causes" and *specific* "effects," as either prescription or proscription. This is the classic formulation of causality within analytical thinking. But this stems from an assumption that the equilibrium of cosmic forces, which permeate the external world, may be disturbed in the act of erecting a building leading to unfavorable consequences ("anything can come from anything"): clearly an instance of mythical causality. However, the solution often prescribed may consist of either orienting the building towards a particular cardinal direction of space or positioning elements of the building, such as openings, columns and so on in a certain prescribed way: the analytical objective thinking with the Cartesian rectilinear grid of space as a tool.

This confusing back and forth between the two views of the world, analytical and mythical, is symptomatic not only of the dominant position the former has come to occupy in the last 300 years but also of the orientalist narrative it has spawned in our march toward modernity. You want to revive and resurrect a thousand-year-old ancestral wisdom but if you think that it can only be represented through categories and tools that are clearly antithetical to that wisdom, you find yourself in an impossible trap. Interestingly, neither *Manasara* nor *Mayamatam*, arguably the two most authentic and surviving texts, attempt to do that. Both maintain their role as the codification of artisanal practices in the same way as the work of Vitruvius. For example, describing columns and their properties, *Architecture of Manasara* states, "*Jangha, charana, stali, stambha, anghrika, sthanu, sthuna, pada, skambha, arani, bharaka* and *dharana*: these are the twelve successive synonyms (of pillars) as stated by the ancients."[9] Further down, we are given more details:

> (When) the whole length of the upper portion (i.e., entablature) is equal to the portion ending at the neck (i.e., capital), and the middle portion (i.e., shaft), which is uniformly fluted, is equal to that (i.e., the combined height of the entablature and the capital) and is twice the lower portion (i.e., the base); and the remaining bottom portion (i.e., the pedestal), which should be made quadrangular in shape, is equal to the latter (i.e., the base); that pillar is called the *Chitra-kantha*; it should be employed in all kinds of buildings.[10]

Elsewhere, in *Mayamatam*, we find the following:

> The intercolumniation should be from two to four cubits which, if six digits are added each time, gives nine possibilities. After a suitable intercolumniation has been chosen it is to be used for all the pillars of any one building no matter what is the type. *If the disposition of the pillars is irregular this will bring destruction upon the building and upon the site but, if the whole arrangement is true to the principle, success will ensue.*[11]

(italics mine)

It is clear from above that the specific instructions in both these texts fall within the category of received wisdom of best practices "as stated by the ancients." But the last line refers to the ultimate aim of it all, that is, proper and thoughtful distribution of energy throughout the building, which will remain constant.

Apparently, it seems that the practice of *Vaastu* existed at two levels in Vedic and Upanishadic times: at the immediate level of those engaged in the actual practice of designing and erecting buildings, the *shilpis* (craftsmen) and at the higher level of the *sthapatis* (architects). At the immediate level, the texts provided the guidelines covering almost all operations involved in erecting a building. These were based on the accumulated experiences and wisdom of their forefathers, which had come to them through the oral tradition ("as stated by the ancients") but was variable and liable to evolve with new experiences. At a more distant level, the larger philosophical view of the enfolding, unbroken universe, the *shrutis* provided the constant anchor to which all actions can be pegged. The *sthapati* was responsible for negotiating the two levels. In actual practice, texts containing ancient wisdom may not always be of help in moral dilemmas because they themselves are often in conflict with one another. That is why one needs intelligence (*buddhi*), learning (*vidya*) and training in *pramanas* (means of knowledge), to interpret the knowledge derived from handed-down tradition. An architect's code of conduct (*dharma*) cannot be intellectually blind and uncritical. Earlier (Chapter 3) we had referred to *sabda* (word or scriptures) as a source of knowledge. In that context, Mohanty makes an important distinction between facts and values: "scriptures impart knowledge of ethical truths about what one ought to do, and in that sense, of values, while of facts the scriptures, or *sabda*, are not an independent source of knowledge." He then goes on to state that:

it would be a mistake to correlate the distinction between *sabda* as a *pramana* and the other *pramanas* with the distinction generally made between value and fact . . . The question was if the same facts about which *sabda* can yield knowledge are not capable of being known by other means of knowledge. It is this question that led me to assign to *sabda* a unique domain of possible object of knowledge, a domain about which the other means of knowledge cannot generate any knowledge. And this I suggested was *dharma*.[12]

It is not for nothing that *Mayamatam* specifies that the architect be *serva-shastra visharada*, well versed in all forms of knowledge.[13] This is the model of practical rationality I have referred to earlier as Contingent Criticality (Chapter 4).

It has been more than a millennium since this neat arrangement was inter-rupted and almost erased from the collective memory. The transformation of information from the oral to textual form during the *Puranic* period (400 to 1500 CE) first simplified and ritualized much of the Vedic knowledge to make it more accessible to the common people. Two factors seem to be at play here: (1) the early Sanskrit language was highly sophisticated, stylized and not very easy for all to follow. Writing down this oral wisdom into a simpler textual language must have involved interpretations, which may not always carry the spirit of the original. (2) this happened simultaneously with the emergence of the Hindu *Bhakti* movement in response to the increasing popularity of Buddhism. The *Bhakti* (devotion) movement was built around multiple Hindu deities and involved elaborate rituals. Most of the texts which comprise the *Vaastu* litera-ture seem to have been written during this period and can be termed as *Puranic* literature. They may not all be wholly faithful to the subtle nuances of the original. While the *Puranas* aim to complement the Vedic literature, interpret its theories and help spread the ideas therein, some scholars such as Max Muller consider them independent of the Vedic literature, having changed often over its history and having little relation to the Vedic age.[14]

Had they not been interrupted, it is almost certain that the practices would have evolved to incorporate the new ideas, experiences, materials, technolo-gies and ways of inhabitation that every culture incorporates as it grows. This is borne out by the fact that between the ninth and twelfth centuries, during which time the *Mayamatam* seems to have reached its definitive form, it was updated several times. The earliest version prescribed the maximum permissible height of a temple to be twelve storeys but this was later revised to thirteen, fourteen and finally to sixteen storeys to account for the fifteen-storey-high temple, *Brihadeshwara*, at Tanjavur. It is clear that in such matters text (*sabda*) follows the actual practice rather than the other way round. One can be equally sure that this evolution must have happened within the larger philosophical frame-work of the belief in the universe as an enfolding, unbroken whole. For only this sense of wholeness guarantees equilibrium between all forces in nature, avoids conflicts and ensures sustainability. In other words, a living tradition evolved around new facts. The values enshrined in the idea of *dharma* kept it from being fossilized as orthodoxy.

It is interesting that modern science too seems to have accepted the limits of the analytical thinking which for three centuries had assumed that the secrets of the universe can be unraveled by investigating deeper and deeper into the infinite smallness of particle physics. Recent alternative interpretations of quantum theory, on the other hand, are offering the possibility that the concept of the universe as an unbroken whole may offer a better understanding of the riddles of nature.[15]

One of these riddles concerns the idea of indeterminacy. It is normal for us to cling to the belief that our life is completely determined and that all events are linked to some specific causes. As we have seen above, such determinacy, and causality, is central to Western philosophical thinking and has led to the development of modern science and technology. It is also embedded in the deeply entrenched Indian theory of *karma* as a way to bring in some form of determinacy to our lives, although the idea of indeterminacy was always present in Indian thought (*Neti, neti, neti*; Not this, not this, not this). It was only in the early twentieth century that modern science recognized and came to terms with indeterminacy, first through Werner Heisenberg's uncertainty principle in 1927 and then when Kurt Godel's incompleteness theorems challenged the ability of mathematics to be the exemplar of determinate knowledge. Thus, though both came through completely different routes and methods, analytical thought and mythical thought have found convergence in the principle of indeterminacy.

But indeterminacy is not easy to practice in day-to-day life. Could it be that just as people visit sacred places and offer prayers in troubled times, they are similarly responding to the existential problems of contemporary life by interpreting *Vaastu* as a religious text and reposing their faith in its implied determinate causality to solve their present problems? But then, what should we do today with the ancient wisdom contained in the Vedic texts? Taking them as divine wisdom received from beyond would entail dumping all the scientific knowledge gained over the last several centuries, knowledge that has benefited humankind in innumerable ways. Discarding them as outdated and irrelevant, or worse still as superstition, would not only set us adrift without a moral compass but would also negate the unbelievable intellectual achievement of our ancient thinkers. They were no less scientists than what the term implies today. To think that they crafted their ideas about the universe, mathematics, physics and human nature in the absence of the kind of empirical data we take for granted today is an astonishing feat. The answer lies in not posing the issue as that of a polarity between science and faith where one has to choose one of the two. It also lies in understanding the different notions of morality and purpose in the two thought traditions. For Indian thinkers, all the objective and causal laws *had a singular purpose*: that of maintaining and perpetuating the cosmic wholeness and equilibrium. But by not assigning the human agency any independent role in this endeavor, it has led to fatalism; everything is assumed to be pre-ordained. On the other hand, as Steven Pinker argues in a recent article,[16] modern science has established that the laws governing the universe *have no purpose at all*. This lack of intentionality in the laws of nature, as opposed to the Indian view, also implies that we, humankind, are responsible for the consequences of our actions, which may disturb the equilibrium of nature. This view of science is also inherently humanistic and brings in a moral and ethical dimension to science. "This humanism, which is inextricable from a scientific understanding of the world, is becoming the de facto morality of modern democracies, international organizations, and liberalizing religions, and its unfulfilled promises define the moral imperatives we face today."[17]

In other words, this exposes a serious infirmity in mythical thinking when it is interrogated from the opposite shore: analytical thinking is seeking the same equilibrium as sought by mythical thinking but we can no more shirk our responsibilities for having brought the planet to the brink of total annihilation by clinging to fatalism.

So let us ask, is *Vaastu* relevant to us today even though more than a thousand years have passed since it first began to be recorded in textual form? Here I will limit myself to those aspects of this knowledge which impinge on our work as architects. First, we must accept that it is not an instrumental knowledge that can give us ready solutions for our temporal problems. If the entire world is interlinked as an unbroken whole, and "anything can come from anything," why single out architecture alone to explain why our parliament does not function as well as we would like it to? And second, the above brief exploration of mythical thought suggests that everything in this universe, animate and inanimate, is infused with the same energy or spirit which manifests itself as the particular "genius" or spirit of that element or being. A location, a site on which a building is to be erected, will have its "*genius loci*,"[18] incorporating all the existential conditions of its surroundings and which will be different from that of other locations. Thus it is impossible to arrive at a universal prescription of how a building should be located. If the architect in each case is able to tune their own consciousness with this genius of the place, the place itself will reveal how best to proceed. The architect, the building they design, the location, the surroundings and the entire world around will be one unbroken whole.

Similarly, the materiality of a building, the various materials that go into its construction and structural elements, will also have their geniuses telling the craftsmen how to work with them. A good carpenter will always be in tune with the genius of the wood and so will be the mason with that of the brick or stone. This will also apply to modern materials like steel and concrete, which did not exist in ancient times. Nature alone was unable to make these materials but allowed humans to make them, provided they follow nature's laws.

What we thus gather from mythical thinking as relevant to architecture is that, unlike classical science which apprehends a task or an event in space and time as a special instance of a general law, we must approach each task, be it intercolumniation or the placement of a door or window, with a sense of its own will or genius regarding the here and now. This means asking what is the right thing to do, here and now (*desha* and *kala*), which will be sustainable technologically, socially, environmentally, aesthetically and so on. There are no general, determinate and inviolable laws that apply in every situation. There are rules that will have to be interpreted and contextualized in a given situation. This is a task not for a simple craftsman but for an architect who has "crossed the ocean of the science of architecture."[19]

Notes

1 Vitruvius, *The Ten Books on Architecture*, trans. Morris Morgan (New York, Dover Publications, 1960), 17.

2 The present proponents of *Vaastu* never tire of referring to it as an exact science.

3 Ernst Cassirer, *Philosophy of Symbolic Forms*, vol. 2 (New Haven: Yale University Press, 1968), 30.

4 David Bohm. *Wholeness and the Implicate Order* (London: Ark Paperbacks, 1983), x.

5 Ironically, by removing the human agency from this cosmic causality, mythical thinking has given birth to fatalism. Humans are freed from the responsibilities of their own actions which, in today's context, might be detrimental to the survival of the world.

6 Ernst Cassirer, ibid., 46.

7 M. Hirianna, *Outline of Indian Philosophy* (New Delhi: Motilal Banarasidass Publishers, 1993), 56.

8 The interesting twist here is the use of analytical thinking to arrive at this eventuality. We do know now that contacts existed between the Greek, Indian and Mesopotamian cultures as early as the Bronze age, and there were more active exchange of ideas in the Persian Empire. (See Thomas McEvilley, *The Shape of Ancient Thought*. New York: Allworth, 2002.) The idea that the different strands of ancient thought enriched each other opens up vast possibilities for authentic dialog.

9 Prasanna Kumar Acharya, ed. and trans., *Architecture of Manasara* (Delhi: Low Price Publication, 2006), chapter XV, verses 4–6, p. 151.

10 Ibid., chapter XV, verses 26–30, p. 152.

11 Bruno Dagens, ed. and trans., *Mayamatam: Treatise of Housing, Architecture and Iconography* (Delhi: IGNCA and Motilal Banarasidas Publishers, 2000), verses 52–54, pp. 192–193.

12 Jitendra Nath Mohanty, *The Empirical and the Transcendental*, ed. Bina Gupta (Lanham: Rowman & Littlefield, 2000), 276–277.

13 *Mayamatam*, ibid., vol. 1, verse 14, p. 24.

14 Ludo Rocher, *The Puranas* (Wiesbaden: Otto Harrassowitz Verlag, 1986), 13–16.

15 David Bohm and Basil J. Hiley, *The Undivided Universe: An Ontological Interpretation of Quantum Theory* (New York: Routledge, 1993).

16 Steven Pinker, "Science Is Not Your Enemy," *New Republic* (August 7, 2013), available at: https://newrepublic.com/article/114127/science-not-enemy-humanities.

17 Ibid.

18 Christian Norberg-Schulz, *Genius Loci: Towards a Phenomenology of Architecture* (London: Academy Editions, 1980).

19 *Mayamatam*, ibid., vol. 1, p. 27.

Part Three
On Praxis

Chapter 9

Le Corbusier

Polemical, Poetical and Existential

It has been over five decades since Le Corbusier passed away. In historical terms this may not seem a long time. However, a lot has happened during this time and our concerns have moved away from those of the mid-twentieth century. This is confirmed by the fact that while Le Corbusier was alive and for a couple of decades after his death, one could come across some critical writing or commentary about his work. But now it is indeed a rarity to come across a serious critical appraisal of his work, except in academia. Thus these five decades have given us a certain critical distance and a platform of the present context from where we can take a fresh view of the master's ideas and his work.

The term "the present context" implies a certain time span, a period which we usually appropriate for our present. It may be this very moment or the last few decades, but it certainly suggests locating Le Corbusier outside that time span to be brought in during the current discourses for critical review as we seem to be doing now. This is in recognition of the fact that much has indeed changed from the time Le Corbusier practically dominated the modernist discourse in architecture as did Picasso, Mondrian and Klee in painting, Schoenberg in music or Eliot and Joyce in literature. The modernity project was indeed a political project aimed at overturning the classical order, which was seen as non-egalitarian and oppressive. Modernity gave us hope for a better social order based on a different set of values. While we still continue to nurture that hope today, many of the founding assumptions of that project are increasingly being questioned. We now question the universal social order, which ignored the cultural and geographical specificity of communities and sought to unite the whole of humanity on the basis of the single common faculty of reason. We also question the urbanism it entailed which replaced our streets, which were always places of gatherings, with roads, which are elements of mechanized movement, and altered our relationship with the earth. It is ironic that this questioning first began in 1968 in Le Corbusier's Paris by the students of architecture before spreading to other academic centers such as Harvard, Kent State and Columbia University in the USA.

Thus, it is evident that the reaction to the "modernist" dogma had begun only three years after Le Corbusier's death. However, then it was not the historical distance in time that today separates us from Le Corbusier but the very rejection of what he and his contemporaries stood for[1] that distinguishes us in the present from the "past" in which we now locate Le Corbusier.

As such, to view Le Corbusier in the present context leads to interesting readings on at least two levels; at one level it could be read as asking if Le Corbusier has any relevance today. This would be a rather pragmatic and utilitarian approach seeking to uncover if there is anything useful in Le Corbusier for our present tasks. At another level, it can also suggest an exploration of a body of work, half a century old, from the changed perspective of the present time to see if we can discover something that may have remained hidden from us for the last 50 years. This would be a more critical approach and in the process would require that we articulate, or at least outline, what we mean by the "present" as distinct from the past in which we have placed Le Corbusier. I do not mean to suggest here that such an articulation of the "present" be a prerequisite for the exercise, but it will certainly have to emerge as a positive end result of it. We will end up knowing something about ourselves.

History is a funny thing. Historians, as well as critics and commentators who work with historical evidence, usually select from the vast and undifferentiated inventory of past events some of those that can be linked together to construct a coherent "narrative." The events and elements of the past that do not contribute to the "coherence" of the narrative usually get left behind. Thus history, far from being a factual representation of the past, is a human-made cultural construct, for the very process of selection involves *foregrounding* a certain part of the past which then gets etched in our collective consciousness as truth. However, this "foregrounding" characteristic of history also implies that, given a changed perspective and a different ideological lens, the same past may reveal other narratives that may have remained untold but which may receive better reception in different times. A healthy suspicion of history and the concurrent suspension of disbelief in its truism is thus a precondition for going beyond the received wisdom.

I intend to apply this method in giving a second look at Le Corbusier and the context within which he worked. The application of this method itself constitutes an important element of our "present context." The initial task is made relatively easy by the fact that the modernist era, that may have begun with the French Revolution, has been extensively recorded and commented upon by many not only as a coherent cultural and political movement but also with regard to the contributions of many of its heroes, Le Corbusier being one of them. Le Corbusier himself played no small part in this. With his prolific productions, coupled with equally prolific polemics, he pretty much laid down the rules by which he wanted to be understood in history and the terms by which his contemporaries would relate to his work. He consciously projected himself as one who was engaged in ushering in a new world by building its icons. It was a utopian concept founded on industrialization, universality of human reason, the linear and forward march of time, and abstraction. He called it *L'Esprit Nouveau*. He actually went on to establish a visual language, its vocabulary and grammar (Figure 9.1), which was to guide not only artists and architects but also laymen to recognize the simple and abstract geometric relationships with which much of the external world, natural as well as human-made, was organized.

This was Le Corbusier at his polemical best. The historians and critics of the time such as Sigfried Giedion, J.M. Richards, Henry-Russell Hitchcock and Philip Johnson carried forward the development of an ideology that dominated much of

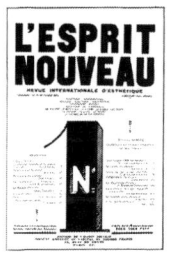
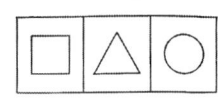
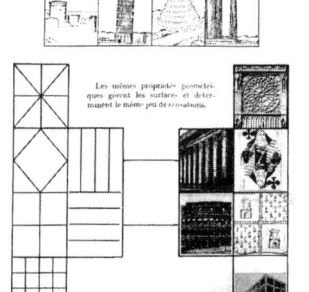

Figure 9.1
Extract from
L'Esprit
***Nouveau.* Le**
Corbusier, Paris,
France, 1920.

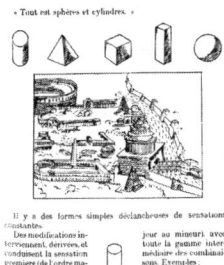

the discourse in architecture in the first half of the twentieth century. It also helped in determining the dominant narrative about Le Corbusier by "foregrounding" some of his projects such as Villa Savoye at Poissy (Figure 9.2), Unité d'Habitation at Marseille (Figure 9.3), the Radiant City (Figure 9.4), the "Modulor," Chandigarh and so on, which supported and exemplified this polemics. So powerful was the "foregrounding" that many of us, if woken up in the middle of the night and asked to list important works of Le Corbusier, would most likely list these.

Figure 9.2
Villa Savoye.
Le Corbusier,
Poissy, France,
1931.

Figure 9.3
**Unité
d'Habitation.
Le Corbusier,
Marseille,
France, 1952.**

Figure 9.4
**The Plan Voisin
de Paris. Le
Corbusier, Paris,
France, 1925.**

And for good reasons. Each of these buildings embodies a part of *L'Esprit Nouveau*. Take Villa Savoye, a house lifted above its grounds. It stands for abstraction and a contextualism. Being a perfect example of the "Five Principles" ("pilotis," "free plan," "free façade," "elongated windows," and "roof garden") it represented an analytical method which seeks to dissect a phenomenon into its component parts to be recombined into different configurations in different contexts (Figure 9.5). It is a building that appeals to the cerebral in us.

Similarly, Unité d'Habitation projected a new form of community and a new form of rational organization consisting of constant structure and variable infill—the rack and the wine bottles, as Le Corbusier described it (Figure 9.6). Le Corbusier also took pains to demonstrate that this building too was made up of component parts which are conceptually independent of each other. The urban projects of the Radiant City and Chandigarh replaced the traditional form of the city—where individual buildings came together, held hands as it were, to form a public realm in the form of streets and well-defined squares and plazas—with wide open spaces populated now by isolated towers. The public realm lost its architectural quality of the past and became an organization of hierarchical movements.

But we need to investigate the nature of these polemics a little more closely. As I have mentioned above, the objective of the polemics was to lead humankind to a utopia away from the oppressive *ancien régime*. On a deeper level though, it stood for (a) analytical thinking, (b) the secularization of culture, (c) the autonomous individual and free enterprise, and (d) democracy. The seeds for this idea were planted in the French Revolution. Over the years, this idea acquired a name—modernity. However, we must distinguish here between modernity and modernism. While the former is an idea, a way of being and doing things, the latter is an ideology, a political position based on an idea that requires a plan of action and is always less than the idea itself. With the hindsight of the last 50 years it is possible to see that while we may question or outright reject

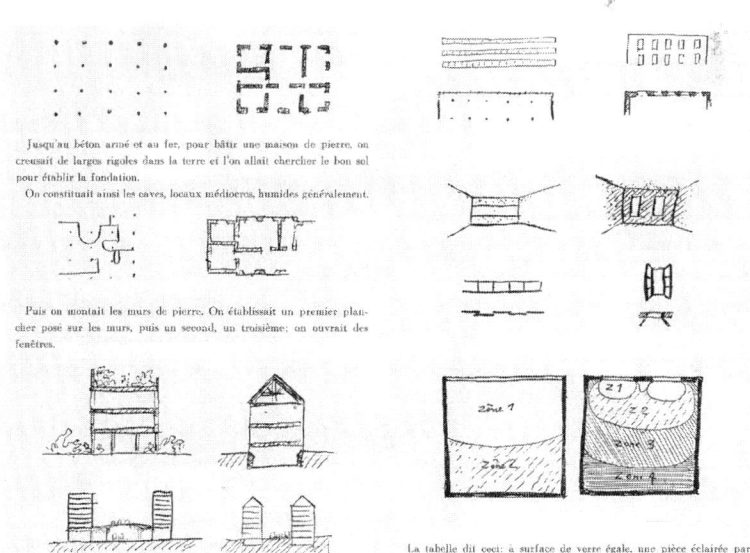

Jusqu'au béton armé et au fer, pour bâtir une maison de pierre, on creusait de larges rigoles dans la terre et l'on allait chercher le bon sol pour établir la fondation.

On constituait ainsi les caves, locaux médiocres, humides généralement.

Puis on montait les murs de pierre. On établissait un premier plancher posé sur les murs, puis un second, un troisième; on ouvrait des fenêtres.

Avec le béton armé on supprime entièrement les murs. On porte les planchers sur de minces poteaux disposés à de grandes distances les uns des autres.

Le sol est libre sous la maison, le toit est reconquis, la façade est entièrement libre. On n'est plus paralysé.

La tabelle dit ceci: à surface de verre égale, une pièce éclairée par une fenêtre en longueur qui touche aux deux murs contigus comporte deux zones d'éclairement: une zone très éclairée; une zone 2, bien éclairée.

D'autre part, une pièce éclairée par deux fenêtres verticales déterminant des trumeaux, comporte quatre zones d'éclairement: la zone 1, très éclairée, la zone 2, bien éclairée, la zone 3, mal éclairée, la zone 4, obscure.

Figure 9.5
The five points for a New Architecture: the pilotis, the free plan, the roof garden, horizontal windows and the free façade. Le Corbusier, Paris, France, 1925.

Figure 9.6
Components of habitation are deconstructed and then reconfigured in a new form. Le Corbusier, Unité d'Habitation, Marseille, France, 1960.

the plans of actions and the prescriptions suggested by the polemical projects of Le Corbusier foregrounded so far, to reject the idea of modernity, as some of the proponents of the so-called "post-modern" seem to propose, will be to throw out the baby with the bath water. These projects, together with many others by Le Corbusier's contemporaries, formed part of a body of work which did exactly what they were supposed to do: to make the world imagine, through them, a society founded on a different set of values. If we see faults in them today, it is only because these buildings, through their presence, helped us gain a critical appreciation of the promise they represented. And promise is always bigger than the prescription.

This is not to suggest the absence of any plastic qualities in these buildings, far from it. Le Corbusier was nothing if not an artist and the sensuous experiences all his buildings offer are second to none. I intend to deal with this a little later. The point here is that the above values these buildings represented—namely abstraction, universality of reason, and conceptual clarity in all human endeavors—comprised the bedrocks of the modernist narrative and had to be *foregrounded*. In the glare of this foregrounding other qualities received less attention at the time. However, now that the luminosity of some of these ideas is fading (though one hopes we do not abandon the modernist project for it still retains much of its validity), it becomes possible to focus our attention on those aspects of Le Corbusier's work which have not received the same intensity of our gaze.

I refer to two projects which represent another aspect of Le Corbusier— the state assembly building at Chandigarh (Figure 9.7) and the unrealized project for the League of Nations at Geneva. It has been widely reported that Le Corbusier's inspiration for the form of the chamber hall at Chandigarh assembly had been the cooling tower of the thermal power station either at Ahmedabad or elsewhere (Figures 9.8 and 9.9). He too has alluded to this in his sketch book. But I believe there is much more to this connection than is obvious. True, the plastic quality of the cooling tower with its simple form and geometry is fascinating but to suggest that Le Corbusier simply borrowed the form because of its plasticity will not be enough. I propose that in this case Le Corbusier was involved in a process that can be described as the "lateral trans-positioning" of an element from its original context to another seemingly unrelated context and in the process investing the element—the cooling tower—with a whole new universe of meanings which were not present in its origin. Simply put, a cooling tower, in its original context, is an ordinary and utilitarian instrument, part of a much larger industrial operation whose function is limited to cooling heated water for its recirculation into the process. In the assembly building it is doing none of this. Instead, by placing it in the context of a political institution of an emerging nation with an aspiration for modernity through industrialization, this industrial element has been elevated as a symbol of the very idea of industrial progress. It has now transcended its original instrumentality and has acquired an iconic status and a representational role for a much bigger idea.

If it was a plastic element in the shape of a cooling tower at the Chandigarh assembly building, in the League of Nations project it was a spatial element that was trans-positioned in a similar way. Giedion has noted the resemblance between the entrance porch at the League of Nations building and a railway platform (Figure 9.10).[2] But again, this does not tell the whole story. Railways,

Figure 9.7
**Palace of
Legislative
Assembly.
Le Corbusier,
Chandigarh,
India,
1953–1963.**

Figure 9.8
**Section, Palace
of Legislative
Assembly.
Le Corbusier,
Chandigarh,
India, 1955.**

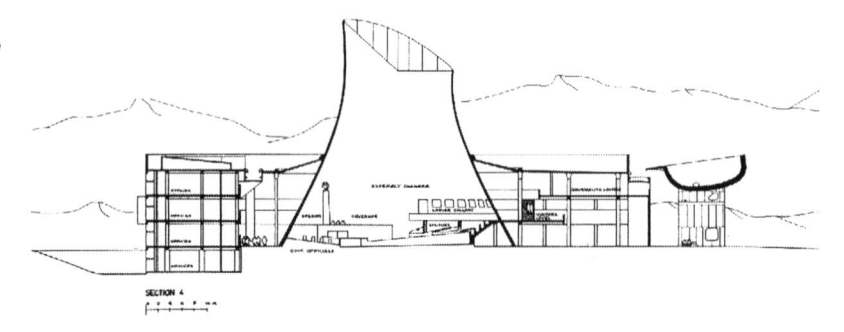

Figure 9.9
**Hyperboloid
towers at
Didcot A Power
Station. Fredrick
Gibberd,
Oxfordshire, UK,
1968.**

of course, were connected with the whole process of industrialization in the nineteenth century and occupied a large part of the popular imagination. Architecture connected with the railways had already given rise to new forms and a language of construction, and had forever altered the relationship between the city and the country. Railway stations also heralded a new social order. Platforms were egalitarian places where people from all walks of life from all parts of the city could gather and be received by the railway to be transported to their respective destinations. This simple linear space of the platform, seemingly utilitarian, was already loaded with multiple meanings: it embodied progress brought about by industrialization, a new democratic social order and new urbanity.

But there already existed a typology for the entrance porch of an important public building (Figure 9.11). It was a grand single space, fronting the main entrance where dignitaries were received one at a time. Only after the previous dignitary has been received and has been ceremoniously escorted inside can another carriage carrying another dignitary occupy the same space. Its occupation was sequential and not simultaneous. Thus conjuring up the image of a simple railway platform at the League of Nations did several things at the same time. Besides the inevitable recollection of the spirit of industrialization and the new emerging suburban middle class, it also referred to a far more equitable and

Figure 9.10
Drawing for the porch, League of Nations.
Le Corbusier, Geneva, Switzerland, 1927.

Figure 9.11
The rotunda and the porch, University of Virginia.
Thomas Jefferson, Charlottesville, VA, United States, 1826.

egalitarian political order where the heads of state and other dignitaries would arrive simultaneously and together with other non-dignitaries.

To be sure, both these projects addressed the same utopia as the other set of projects we discussed earlier. However, there is one crucial difference; while the more polemical projects referred to *L'Esprit Nouveau* in a more direct way and also applied scientific/analytical thinking, these two projects dealt with a more synthetic process to bring together seemingly disparate elements to arrive at a new whole. This is an accepted and recognized function of both visual arts and poetry: to hint at the transcendental with reference to something mundane and of day-to-day familiarity. One—the polemical set—seeks conceptual clarity while the other celebrates perceptual ambiguity.

The oft-quoted and somewhat controversial statement of Le Corbusier that "a house is a machine for living in"[3] should also be seen in this light. The machine it refers to is not just an instrument of industrial production. In one simple stroke, Le Corbusier elevated all the clockworks and cooling towers of the world, all the airplanes, steam engines and ships to a metaphor representing a whole universe of ideas, and a way of life that engendered them. What is not often recognized, however, is that with this statement Le Corbusier altered our relationship with architecture. He placed architecture in the cerebral realm of the mind. Here architecture is to be contemplated and analyzed, it is something on which to hold a viewpoint. This calls for a distinction between viewing and natural seeing. Viewing is when we make an abstract reading of the world, when we say we hold the "world in view" or "worldview" or "viewpoint." Seeing can only happen when we are standing on our feet, at "standpoints." This is a bodily experience and gives us a sense of distance between us and the things of the world. But this distance is not in the air (in abstract measure units such as feet, meters and so on) but in terms of number of paces on the ground to a fixed point, our body. "The world stretches away from a standpoint in both space and time. If we are on our feet in the world, our faces (bodies) will not be loose from the world: they will encompass the world, together-stepping with it."[4]

The movement of our bodies and the things around us jointly make and condition our perception of the world. This is the nature of *existential space*. It is the space of architecture, not the abstraction but the concrete situation in which we conduct our lives. And this cannot be claimed, duplicated, reproduced, contemplated or analyzed.

It may be paradoxical but true that in spite of all the polemical posturing and in spite of coining the slogan "a house is a machine for living in," Le Corbusier was never far from the existential in his architecture. It is we who have missed consciously experiencing it. Look at two more projects, the chapel at Ronchamp (Figure 9.12) and the Dominican monastery at La Tourette (Figure 9.13). Both of these buildings are considered the two least polemical of Le Corbusier's work. In fact they have been thought of as not part of the mainstream body of his work and instead personal expressions of a creative genius. However, such an impression may be a result of the "foregrounding" I referred to earlier which has so conditioned the collective consciousness of a whole generation as to eclipse our attention on qualities that surely existed in all of Le Corbusier's works but are in especially abundant supply in these two religious buildings.

Since our search is for the perceptual/existential qualities more than the cognitive ones, we will have to devise a method that relies more on natural seeing, rather than abstract viewing, and allow our bodies, standing on our two feet, to be encompassed and enveloped by the elements of the buildings. The images we gather will naturally be a series of partial images, limited by the scope of our perceptual capacities and not an overall grand image of the whole at a time. We shall replace the "mind's eye view" with the "retinal view."

Figure 9.12
The Chapel of Notre Dame du Haut. Le Corbusier, Ronchamp, France, 1955.

Figure 9.13
Sainte Marie de La Tourette. Le Corbusier, Eveux, France, 1957.

As we walk through the building it does not unfold but enfolds us. The spaces acquire characteristics that are contingent upon our presence within; they lose independent meanings. In the words of John Schumacher, architecture is "co-made" by the building and the observer. Quality of light shapes our perception to a large extent (Figure 9.14). It determines the sense of confinement and release (Figure 9.15). The materiality of the walls, with their rough texture, make us acutely aware of the distance between them and our shoulders (Figure 9.16). It makes us aware of our physical being. It makes us the center, the vanishing point of a scene which changes as we move.[5] This blurs the distinction between the subject and the object.

Such an experiential relationship with architecture is not replicable from one observer to another. In fact, neither the above description nor photographic representation will replace the actual experience. It is precisely this reason—that such a view of architecture is subjective and cannot be objectively represented for public discourse—that may have prevented these qualities of Le Corbusier's architecture being brought to the fore in most of the twentieth century's discourse, which so heavily leaned toward objectivity. But we may be more receptive to this now

Figure 9.14
Interior of the Ronchamp Chapel.

Figure 9.15
The haptic space of the Chapel at La Tourette.

Figure 9.16
**Light, the
texture of the
walls and the
dimensions
all add to the
experiential
quality of
this chapel.
Le Corbusier,
La Tourette,
France, 1957.**

than before and with this changed receptivity we need to give Le Corbusier a second look. I have walked through Villa Savoye and the Mill Owner's building in Ahmedabad, with this new perspective, and have not been disappointed.

Notes

1 See quotation from Giancarlo De Carlo in Chapter 4, this volume.
2 Sigfried Giedion, *Space, Time and Architecture* (Cambridge, MA: Harvard University Press, 1962), 523.
3 Le Corbusier, *Towards a New Architecture* (New York: Dover Publications, 1986), 4.
4 John Schumacher, *Human Posture: The Nature of Inquiry* (New York: SUNY Press, 1989), 166.
5 For a much better exploration of this phenomenon, although in a different context, see Stella Kramrisch, *A Survey of Paintings in The Deccan* (New Delhi: Orient Reprint, 1983), 4–8.

Chapter 10

Analogs of Architecture

Not much is known about the history of model making in the practice of architecture. A few stray references here and there tell us that while it is taken for granted that making models and presenting one's designs through models is an established part of normal architectural practice, not much thought is given to the role of models in the *actual process* of designing. With curiosity I tried to browse the Web to find out if anyone has done this, only to be confronted with a long list of people and organizations that would make a model for someone else for a price. Apparently there is a trend now to "parcel out" even this from the normal practice.

There is an interesting reference in the fifteenth-century architect and theorist Leon Battista Alberti's treatise on architecture *De Re Aedificatoria*. Alberti commended the

> ancient custom of builders, who not only in draughts and paintings, but in real models of wood or other substance, examin'd and weigh'd over and over again . . . the whole work and admeasurements of all its parts, before they put themselves to the expence or trouble.[1]

Clearly, for Alberti, the purpose of making a model was to *examine and weigh over and over again* all his decisions while they were being made and not to present that model to clients or others.

Today, more than any other objective, we understand models as elements of *presentation*, that is to say, they are scaled-down three-dimensional replicas of a proposed building to present to a lay person a realistic impression of what the building will look like. Drawing alone cannot do this as drawings, especially two-dimensional ones, constitute an abstract language, a system of codification of the reality into a language of lines, which makes a drawing several steps removed from that reality; not an easy task for a lay person to understand. Sketches and other rendered images are a bit closer but the problem with these is that they represent the reality of the project in a partial way and that too in a way that the architect, more often than not, wants us to see. It is like the architect is putting their best foot forward. A model can overcome this limitation. It allows one to move around, albeit like a bird hovering over a city, and take in the whole, stopping and pondering on the way as one likes it.

But then one cannot help being curious. Why didn't Alberti mention presentation as a reason for making a model? You see, Alberti and his contemporaries in the early fifteenth century were not yet used to drawing realistic perspectives. In fact Alberti himself contributed in no small measure toward the invention of perspective drawings but the technique was not yet that widely used. He did not send a model to Ludovico, patron of the Benedictine Abbey of Sant'Andrea in Mantua from whom he was angling for a project to rebuild this church (it turned out to be one of his finest). He sent a sketch saying "It will be more capacious, more lasting, more worthy, more cheerful. It will cost much less."[2] All these qualities could easily have been conveyed more forcefully through a model, which as we learnt earlier, he knew all about from the ancients.

My guess is that convincing the client was not such a high priority in his scheme of things, although historians tell us[3] that at least one wooden model of Sant'Andrea was built but it has not survived the ravages of time. There may have been others. How did Alberti arrive at those magnificent proportions of Sant'Andrea that make this building stand apart from all the others built at that time? How did he choose all those elements of his composition whereby nothing can be altered without changing the whole? Did it all come out in one single creative rush or did he have to struggle like most of us usually do? If so, what instruments did he use to show him the way?

I propose that Alberti's architecture, like all great architecture, was built upon a succession of models, each one being an instrument of inquiry. The point is that the role of models was, and has always remained, internal to the process of designing, as opposed to being a tool of marketing, which is external to designing. The act of making design choices depended upon the designer critically evaluating those choices with the help of analogous replicas.

The very act of conceptualizing an idea and crystallizing it into temporal forms is a far more complex process than we realize. It is synchronic and cyclical in nature as opposed to diachronic and linear as in the case of engineering problem solving. Such a process requires a catalyst—a metaphor or a model—that can trigger a revelation. In other words, a designer is not expected to start with a clear knowledge of what they are looking for—a *sense* maybe but not knowledge, which calls for a clearly definable, a priori statement of an idea. Nor is the designer aware of what may guide their choices. Remember Le Corbusier's famous proposition, "Creation is a patient search?" I believe what he meant by this was that an artist is searching for that sense of order and this search ends precisely at the moment they arrive at an image, which shows them in temporal form what they have been searching for. Thus the *making of the image* precedes the *articulation of the idea*. The making itself is the search and it follows no logical path. It is full of exploration, struggle and frustration requiring patience. It is in this search, the process rather than the product, that we locate the role of models in architecture.

This may be illustrated with Kahn's project for the Performing Arts Center at Fort Wayne (Figures 10.1 and 10.2). Both the first series of sketches as well as the sequence of models show an intense search for that clarity which will inform architectural choices. It is arrived at through simultaneous explorations in plans and through models. Each of the plans in the sequence as well as the models seems to reveal an unexpected aspect of the space and gradually clarify what one is looking for. Kahn once told this author that the central courtyard—the Plaza of

Entrances—revealed itself through this process only. When the clarity is reached, the restlessness of the earlier sketches/models is replaced by a confident order whereby everything has found a place and an inevitable position within the whole.

It all comes down to the method of working. Method is linked to the nature of the activity, in this case architecture, and the way it is represented in our consciousness. Do we represent architecture as a scientific, logical, problem-solving, technical activity, or do we represent it as a design activity, with a technical component in its training and working and which, through the built environment in the forms of either buildings or cities, seeks to convey an idea of order or of a society? At the end of the day, both technology and architecture produce tangible images and are informed by ideas and concepts. However, the difference between the two is important in the context of our present inquiry on the role of models, as models are part of that relationship between images and concepts.

Figure 10.1
Initial explorations through sketches. Louis I. Kahn, Fort Wayne Performing Arts Center, 1961.

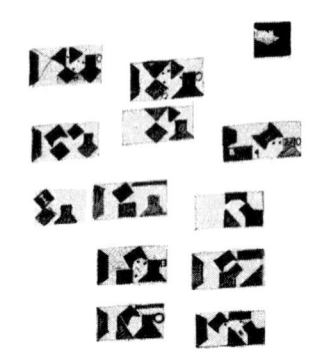

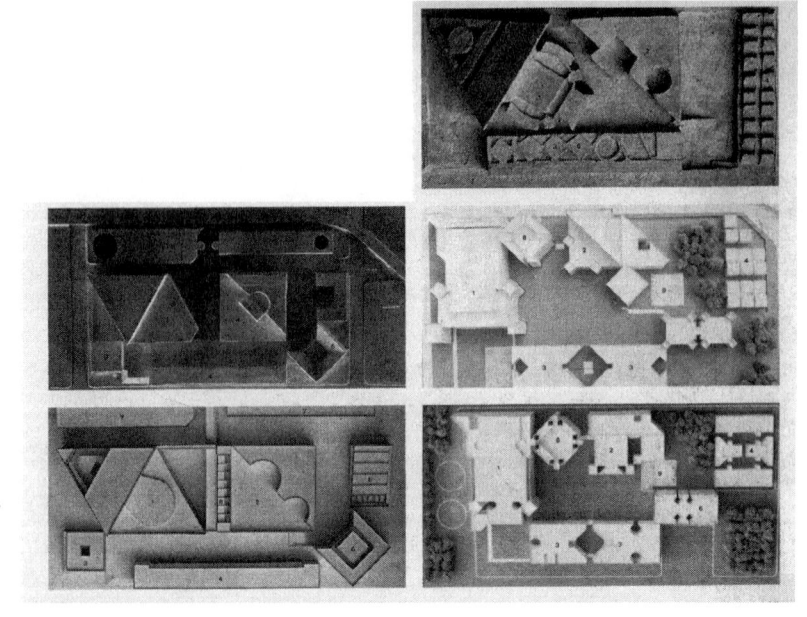

Figure 10.2
Initial explorations through models. Louis I. Kahn, Fort Wayne Performing Arts Center, 1961.

The methods employed by science and technology on the one hand and the creative arts on the other are diametrically opposed to each other in their relationship between the concepts and the tangible, corporeal forms produced by both. While science begins with ideas and concepts and, through technology, seeks to create objects and events (transformation of the physical environment), the arts seek to project an idea (of order, unity) through corporeal forms.[4] In other words, "thinking" and "doing" stand in different relationships in science and in the arts.

Most of us are conditioned to think before doing anything. But in the arts the sequential relationship between thinking and doing is often reversed. An architect often explores through a sketch or a model (doing) and then ponders about its consequences (thinking). Doing precedes thinking or rather they both are reciprocal and feed off each other. It is a *reflective action*, an action that critically reflects upon itself, and design action, which is both a cause as well as a consequence of a well-considered critical evaluation of its suitability and supportability in a given situation. This critical evaluation does not come in the abstract. In fact imagination is never stimulated in the abstract; it needs a concrete image.

And it is here that models (and also sketches) play an important role by being catalysts to focus this reflective action. They are the mirrors that reflect an architect's sub-conscious intentions, making them aware of their implications and taking that "patient search" a step or two further. Thus we locate the role of models firmly within the act of designing itself: as necessary tools of inquiry, investigation and exploration of a designer's intentions before they are crystallized in real space. Models for presentation and for communicating to the client/patron may still be needed but they do not substitute for models as tools of reflection. In other words, architecture can ill afford to represent itself as a purely rational activity with a linear and analytical method terminating with an image or an object only at the end. Such a representation challenges the very identity and the objective of the activity we call architecture. This is not to imply that design is devoid of rationality; rationality in design has a far more complex role.

The making of the model itself offers interesting clues to this complexity. Even though a model is analogous to a building in its image, constructing the model is an entirely different proposition from constructing the actual building. "Fabricating" a model, as it were, with plainer materials such as cardboard, forces one to simplify the complexity of the design to its essential corporeal elements. On the other hand, "sculpting" a model in clay, plaster, wood or stone offers one a perception of the building's wholeness, which transcends material differences and articulations. The complete absence of resistance that relatively new materials such as foam plastic offer, makes explorations of design possibilities almost effortless, allowing the architect much greater freedom and ease of working. Once the hesitation caused by material resistance is removed, a designer may feel free to explore possibilities that they may have avoided earlier. Either way, in the very act of making a model, one gains invaluable insights into the nature of the work which cannot be had in the absence of this important tool. In all these various ways of making a model, there is always an element of cerebral engagement. Rationality manifests itself in more ways than one.

Unfortunately, a large part of the contemporary practice, and also the training of architects, has devalued this part of the process of designing. And this had begun even before the advent of computers, which are believed to have provided an easy alternative to physical models. Computers have changed the way architecture is produced but their impact as tools of representation has not yet been properly understood. They do have a profound effect on the way we look at the world around us, opening up unforeseen possibilities; that is, the transparency implied in the unhidden "wire frame" model has the potentiality to change the way we perceive space—something that neither of the traditional materials can do. In any case they will not, and should not, replace the physical tools of representation, which constitute sketches and models. Ideally, computers should be seen as providing another way of seeing your work. Who knows, they may still broaden and enrich the inquiry.

It is obvious that, over the last two centuries, a significant displacement of the objective of architecture has taken place from that of building "good" buildings to, at first, "useful" buildings and then later merely "beautiful" buildings. Whereas "good" implies both aesthetic and ethical dimensions rolled into one, both "useful" and "beautiful" are strictly speaking apolitical and extra moral. Yet according to that sensitive architect Romaldo Giurgola, in architecture ethics is just as inescapable in art, and the "beautiful" and the "good" are "inextricably joined in the same practical system which provided the basis both for the *construction of buildings and the creation of a work of art*" (italics mine).[5] In other words, rational and non-rational co-existed in the same work.

That changed in 1747 when a Frenchman by the name of Perronet established, for the first time in history, a School of Civil Engineering. Until then the term "architect" implied both a builder, well versed in the craft of construction and engineering, as well as an artist. With this seemingly innocuous event architecture seems to have suffered its first crisis of confidence. What was taken for granted earlier as inseparable—namely, the construction of buildings and the creation of a work of art—was now divided into two separate compartments, each with its own independent practitioner. The representation of architecture and civil engineering as two separate disciplines with their own methods and myths replaced the earlier unified whole. Civil engineering defined for itself and occupied the space of measurable rationality while architecture, by default, had to contend with its opposite, namely the immeasurable and indefinable.

The crystallization of the popular perception of architecture as a quasi-technical activity happened gradually from then on. Beginning with the revolutionary romanticism of Boullee and Ledoux to the rationalism of Viollet-le-Duc, Henri Labrouste and Auguste Choisy, to the Arts and Crafts of William Morris and finally ending up in the functionalism of the twentieth century, architecture went through a series of changes in definition, in search of a new identity. The process of designing took on the qualities of a logical, step-by-step, problem-solving method when architects, looking for legitimacy, felt that they too, like engineers, must be accountable to the strictly rational qualities of the mind. Architecture came to be perceived more as a technical activity than a design activity.

Measurable efficiency replaced expression of order as the objective of architecture and rational, linear analysis displaced the patient search.

One does not have to go too far to see what this means. Look at our schools. How many of them stress, in their pedagogy, the need for designing through exploration? Such explorations demand that initially we challenge the students to explore a number of possibilities, without prior authorization of directions favored by the faculty or by prevailing convensions. Such pedagogy requires constantly working in three dimensions through models.

There are still a significant number of architects who still hold on to the tradition, though. The present exhibition[6] of models done in the studio of Balkrishna Doshi is a welcome opportunity to reaffirm the faith. It is entirely appropriate to see Doshi's work here for he has been closely associated with both Le Corbusier and Louis Kahn. Studios of both these masters were always filled with hundreds of models, small and big, at various stages of evolution of the projects, all of them evidence of the often bloody struggle that design exploration is all about. All were dedicated to the task of making "good architecture first and foremost."

Seeing the large *oeuvre* of Doshi's work on display here and the general issues raised above prompts me to situate the present exhibition at the confluence of two disparate but interconnected issues. These are (1) the process which results in architectural production as it encompasses both art and construction, and (2) the crisis of identity of the profession in the context of, especially in India, its inability to produce architectural exemplars of the ongoing and unresolved dialectic debate between the modernist aspirations on one side and the traditional sensibilities on the other.

Doshi's intellectual and professional biography helps us navigate through these. Coming from a family closely linked to artisanal activity of furniture making, Doshi's initiation into architecture happened at the neo-classical Sir J.J. School of Architecture at Mumbai (Bombay), followed by an internship at the *atelier* of Le Corbusier at a time when all of Europe was seized by the modernist frenzy of post-war rebuilding. He returned to India just in time to participate in the Nehruvian grand project of building the "New Temples" of the newly independent, full-of-hope, nation state. In the early 1960s Doshi came in contact with Louis Kahn and this association lasted until the death of the master in 1975. Thus, Doshi has been strategically placed to be able to actively engage with the current search for the new identity of architecture liberated from its Euro-centricity and also to help create visible images of India, fast modernizing but still incorporating its traditional sensibilities.

Taken individually, each project's evolution seems clearly linked to the explorations carried out through both sketches and models. Where projects are seen to evolve through a sequence of proposals, the direction of exploration is towards clarity and simpleness (as opposed to simplicity). I refer particularly to the projects for "Sangath," "Gujarat Labour Institute," "Gufa," "Manisha House" and "Ompuri" at Matar. These are of particular interest in view of the points made earlier about models. Here materials appropriate for each model have successfully achieved different expressions of the same idea. Complex interpenetration of volumes resulting in equally complex surfaces is studied quickly through the use of materials such as foam plastic, clay or wood.

Beginning with Sangath (Figures 10.3 and 10.4), Doshi seems to be taking more and more liberty with geometry. Whereas in the Gandhi Labor Institute (Figure 10.5), the ultimate resolution seems to be constrained by the inherent geometry of the vault, in Sangath the simple linearity of the vault provides an effective counterpoint to a complex spatial organization at floor level. This includes

Figure 10.3
Model in wood. B.V. Doshi, Sangath, architect's own office, Ahmedabad, 1981. Notice the articulation of the ground plane.

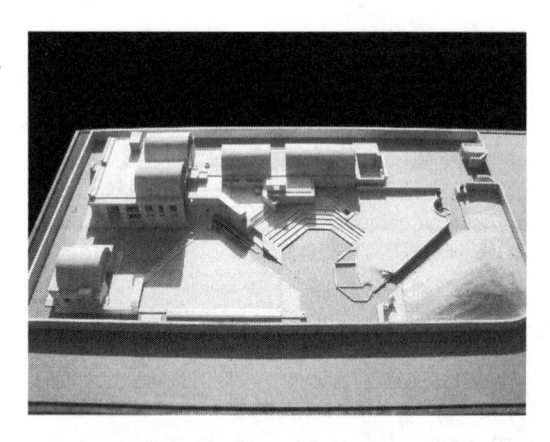

Figure 10.4
Detail study through model. B.V. Doshi, Sangath, architect's own office, Ahmedabad, 1981.

Figure 10.5
Model in clay. B.V. Doshi, Gandhi Labor Institute, Ahmedabad, 1980–1984.

the grounds outdoors, with their multiple levels, as well as the various components of a working studio inside. The simpleness, which does not preclude complexity, of the final solution has been arrived at through a series of three-dimensional studies as is evident from the models.

It is in the later projects, such as NIFT, Gufa (Figure 10.6), the Diamond Bourse at Mumbai (Figure 10.7) and a few small residences, especially the Manisha House (Figure 10.8) and Tejal House (Figure 10.9) that one can see Doshi challenging the tyranny of geometry more confidently. More than any-where else such an enterprise requires ceaseless studies and testing of one's assumptions through the three-dimensional medium of models. The resulting forms are full of surprises.

Take for example Gufa (Figure 10.10). The inner cave-like space has no beginning and no end. The space is articulated more through light than through

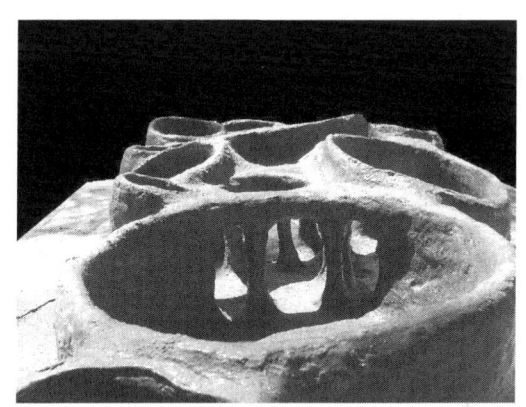

Figure 10.6
**Clay model
without the
domed tops.
B.V. Doshi, Gufa,
Ahmedabad,
1992–1995.**

Figure 10.7
**Model in hard
wood and glass.
B.V. Doshi,
Bharat Diamond
Bourse,
Mumbai, 1998.
Solid glass is
used to express
the diamond-
like extremities
of the buildings.**

Figure 10.8
**Study model in
foam plastic.
B.V. Doshi,
Manisha House,
Vadodara, 2001.**

Figure 10.9
**Detail, study
model in
foam plastic.
B.V. Doshi,
Tejal House,
Vadodara, 1992.**

Figure 10.10
**Interior view
of the cave-like
gallery. Painted
ceiling and
artworks by
M.F. Husain,
B.V. Doshi,
Gufa, 1994.**

geometry. While walking on the floor, which itself is not flat and horizontally leveled, one's sense of gravity and stability is challenged. In other words it is a sensuous space, a space in the co-making, which demands a whole body in experiencing it and not just the visual faculty.

Similarly, the sharp, crystalline quality of the Diamond Bourse complex as it meets the sky is reminiscent of the expressionist architecture of Erich Mendelsohn. Apart from their non-simple geometry, architectural projects like the Diamond Bourse as well as the Gufa require concrete analogous images to discipline their making and resolve various details without which they cannot come into being. In the final analysis, architecture must be made and experienced in the real physical world and must be accountable to the laws of nature in its making.

Usually, architectural exhibitions present comprehensive information on each of the projects presented. In such cases models constitute a part of the larger narrative of project information. Seeing them largely removed from that narrative and independent of the drawing and photographs of the buildings themselves, as in this exhibition, one is prompted to see them as independent objects of art. They have now transcended their utilitarian and representational value as replicas of something else and have acquired a life of their own. While their beginning is firmly rooted in the context of their respective project brief, they now offer a way of looking at the purely architectural qualities of the model unencumbered by the program that generated it. This may result in unexpected revelations. The transparency of the glass model for the Kanoria project in Ahmedabad clearly illustrates this (Figure 10.11).

It is not my intention here, nor is it appropriate, to explain or interpret the models on display in this exhibition; they speak for themselves. In their own way, the models themselves, each one of them, are far more eloquent testimonials of Doshi and his team's ceaseless pursuit of *good* architecture. Still, it is important to restate that models, as analogs of architecture, are an inseparable part of the process of design and not merely tools of presentation.

Figure 10.11
**Model in
plexiglass
and wood.
B.V. Doshi,
the Kanoria
Centre for Arts,
Ahmedabad,
1983.**

Notes

1 Leone Batista Alberti, *The Ten Books of Architecture*, trans. James Leoni, ed. Joseph Rykwert (London: Alec Tiranti, 1965), 22.

2 Joseph Rykwert and Martin Charles, "Sant'Andrea, Mantua," *The Architects' Journal*, 183(21) (May 1986), 38.

3 Heather Horton, "Alberti, Sant'Andrea in Mantua," *Khan Academy*, available at: https://www.khanacademy.org/humanities/renaissance-reformation/early-renaissance1/sculpture-architecture-florence/a/alberti-santandrea-in-mantua.

4 Claude Lévi-Strauss, *The Savage Mind* (Chicago: University of Chicago Press, 1968), 22.

5 Romaldo Giurgola, "Notes on Architecture and Morality," *Precis*, 2 (1980), 51.

6 This essay was first written for the catalogue of the exhibition of Mr. Doshi's models.

Chapter 11

Romaldo Giurgola
The Reluctant Master

Philadelphia in the 1960s was an exciting place to be for a young architect and I was fortunate to be there between 1965 and 1975. The Graduate School of Fine Arts at the University of Pennsylvania seemed to be where all the action was. Dean Perkins at the school had gathered a remarkable group of people who not only mutually supported each other but also, through their work and ideas, sustained an atmosphere of expectancy that something new was in the making and that one cannot just sit back and relax. The people who gathered to nurture this fertile ground included Louis Kahn, Romaldo Giurgola, Robert Venturi and Robert Geddes in architecture, Edmund Bacon and David Crane in urban design, Ian McHarg in landscape architecture, Denise Scott Brown in planning, and the brilliant French engineer Robert Le Ricolais and the urban sociologist Herbert Gans.

The city of Philadelphia itself had also had a strong architectural and urban planning tradition. William Penn's plan of the city, locating it at the narrowest land between the gentle curves of two rivers, with its five squares and the diagonal Benjamin Franklin Parkway designed by Paul Philippe Cret and Jacques Greber, made it one of the most comprehensible cities in America (Figure 11.1). While Paul Cret had introduced Philadelphia to the strong French Beaux-Arts tradition, Frank Furness had experimented with the peculiarly American tectonic tradition of brick, wood and cast iron with a number of remarkable buildings in and around the city (Figures 11.2 and 11.3). In 1932 George Howe and William Lescaze had built, on the Market Street in the center of the city, the PSFS building (Figure 11.4), the first International Style tower in America.

Thus, around 1960, both the city with its historical tradition, which can only be described as non-singular (Cret, Furness and Howe) and the Graduate School of Fine Arts at the University of Pennsylvania, with a group of restless minds looking for a new direction, were ready to embark on arguably one of the most influential decades in the history of contemporary architecture. The result of this synthesis was a movement loosely identified as the "Philadelphia School," which can be seen as an unique confluence of the city and its architectural traditions, architectural practice of a group of architects and the education of architecture and urbanism which flowered at the University of Pennsylvania in the two decades between 1955 and 1975. I want to argue here that the "Philadelphia School," together with the "Team 10" group in Europe, constituted the most serious critique of the then prevalent conventional wisdom of modernism.

Figure 11.1
**Jacques
Gréber's 1917
partial plan of
the city showing
its new civic
center and the
connection of
the Fairmount
Parkway.**

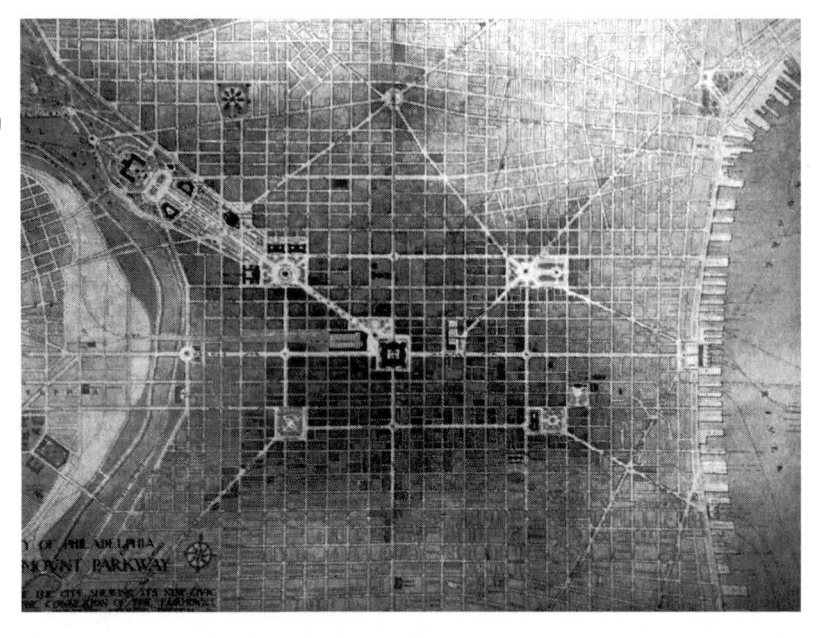

Figure 11.2
**Main Reading
Hall. Frank
Furness,
Furness Library,
University of
Pennsylvania,
Philadelphia,
USA, 1891.**

It is within this unique context that I want to explore the evolving career of Romaldo Giurgola and interrogate his work, which constituted the clearest challenge to modernist conventions.

Louis Kahn was indeed the undisputed leader of this group. His work, especially the Richards Laboratory in Philadelphia and the Trenton Community Center, had opened up the possibility of an alternative narrative. And while all the

Figure 11.3
**Glen Mills
Railway Station**.
**Frank Furness,
Glen Mills,
Pennsylvania,
USA, 1882.**

Figure 11.4
**PSFS Building,
George Howe,
Philadelphia,
USA, 1932.**

younger disciples had pursued their own directions, this relationship between the master and the disciple is most complex in the case of Romaldo Giurgola (Aldo to his colleagues).

This relationship revolves around three broad themes: (1) sense of history, (2) sense of the city and (3) secular spirituality of place. The individual biographies of both Kahn and Giurgola before their meeting in Philadelphia as well as the city of Philadelphia itself make this relationship a complex interplay of ideas, ambitions and opportunities. While their respective architecture took on distinctly different expressions and formal resolutions, they shared concerns and values to be expressed and in doing so became effective catalysts for the direction much of contemporary architecture has taken in the following decades. These three themes, then, also provide a framework within which to interrogate the work of Aldo Giurgola.

Sense of History

Perhaps the best way to start is to quote a passage with which Giurgola has introduced Kahn.

> The work of a man is often discussed, analyzed, and studied as the manifestation of a general will. This is particularly true in architecture, which, being eventually considered the tangible evidence of a relationship between events and elements, rests fundamentally on the general aspiration of people to express . . . However, in the study of the work of an artist, two interpretations usually emerge: one in which he is seen as capable of shaping that will, and the other whereby he becomes the catalyser of that will.
>
> The acceptance of either one of these interpretations becomes less and less appropriate when his work is no longer taken as the synthesis of a historical process but simply as the consequence of a human force, conscious of its own intentions. Much of great architecture is the result of this consequence . . .
>
> This does not occur simply because a formal synthesis is obtained, but, rather, because a comprehensive idea of order is validated . . .
>
> Thus he is a person willing and capable of taking that risk for a better and more conscious world, fully knowing that its future is not attained lying in the sun. It must be painstakingly built upon the present. Louis Kahn was such a person.[1]

There is something very significant in this passage. Giurgola starts by first establishing a normative condition under which human endeavors are generally understood as part of a historical process, in the true Hegelian sense, as expressions of the general will. But then, having established a normative condition, he goes on to state that it is inappropriate to try to locate or interpret Louis Kahn as part of this historical process. Even Kahn himself had hinted at his own peculiar relationship with history when he located himself at the "volume zero" of history; outside and beyond its dialectic. But this passage also indicates a possible hint of how Giurgola himself perceived his own relationship with Kahn. It is significant to note that before arriving in Philadelphia Giurgola's architectural ideas had already been formed by his early life in the classical and pre-modernist urban environment of Italy and his subsequent training as an architect in Rome. This seems to have given him a sense of history second to none. History not as a sequence of events but as a totality of those events, asking not for the reasons why something happened but looking for the meanings embodied in the forms humans have built throughout history. While this sense of history has led Aldo to rightly understand Kahn's work not as "the synthesis of a historical process," it also at once makes him locate himself and his own work as part of the normative conditions of the historical synthesis but still closer to Kahn. Giurgola seems to use himself as a foil against which to sharply see the contours of another architect and also visa versa with equal reciprocity. This provides us with a unique perspective to see Giurgola's work at a time when architecture's relationship with history was at best confusing: Bauhaus had rejected history as an impediment to innovation but still, the Lincoln Center was built in New York city with clear reference to classicism.

Sense of the City

Giurgola's urbanism, distinctly European and pre-modern, leads to a multi-layered relationship with both Kahn and the city of Philadelphia. In the early 1960s Louis Kahn was invited, as a consultant, to the Philadelphia City planning Commission, then headed by Edmund Bacon, to prepare a plan for the development of the city center. Kahn, skirting all historical knowledge about the idea of the city, built over centuries, plunged deep into his own consciousness to redefine the city, street and its institutions and came up with his iconic design with marine metaphors of rivers, harbors, canals and docks to describe various elements of the city (Figure 11.5). But Bacon rejected this as too removed from the reality of the city. Bacon then asked Giurgola, who, anchoring himself firmly in history, chose to carry on from where Paul Cret had left off. His proposal for the Eastern part of the Market Street matches Cret's Parkway (Figure 11.6) in terms of both scale and grandeur. While Paul Cret connected the center of the city with the North Western suburbs with his Champs-Élysées-like Grand Boulevard, Giurgola connected the city center with the historic Independence Mall and the urban residential section of Society Hill near the Delaware River with a long running urban concourse one level below the street (Figure 11.7). While both these schemes, by Kahn and Giurgola, differed in their historical referencing as well as in resolution, they both nonetheless raised serious questions about the direction twentieth-century urbanism had taken.

Fragmentation of the integrated urban fabric into clearly defined zones of activities such as residential, commercial, recreational and so on, and reducing the urban form into the binary of isolated towers and open space, had deprived the post-war cities of their identity and placeness. Streets, once thought of as

Figure 11.5
**Proposal for Pen
Center East,
Philadelphia.
Louis I. Kahn,
Philadelphia,
USA, 1956–1962.**

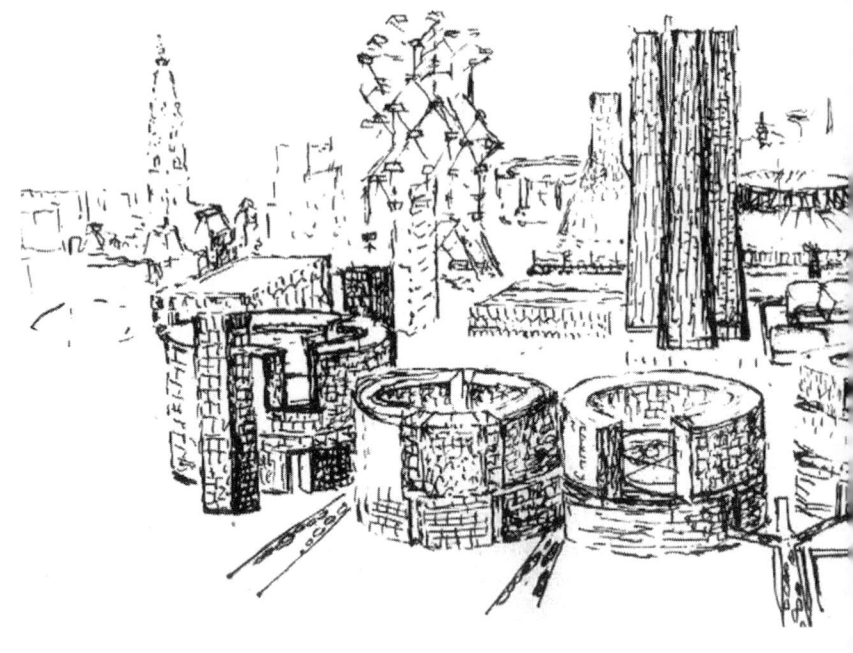

Figure 11.6
**Benjamin
Franklin
Parkway,
looking at the
City Hall Tower
from the porch
of the museum,
Philadelphia,
USA.**

Figure 11.7
**Sectional
Perspective,
Market Street
East proposal.
It contained
an enclosed
shopping,
parking and
transportation
hub in addition
to offices.
Romaldo
Giurgola,
Philadelphia,
USA, 1963.**

places of gathering, were now arteries filled with automobiles going from one zone to another. The inner cities, once a paradise for pedestrians, were now fast losing their attraction for residents. Both the proposals of Kahn and Giurgola had posed a serious critique of this urbanism by reaffirming their faith in the inner city. Though neither proposal was realized, today one finds traces of Giurgola's plan in the eastern part of Market Street where it is connected with the rejuvenated Society Hill.

Secular Spirituality of the Place

Both Kahn and Giurgola have been searching for what I call the "Spirituality of the Place" in architecture, conspicuously absent in all the modernist discourse so concerned with abstraction, the glorification of technology and functions, and self-referential buildings. Here again clues about what this means are to be found in what Giurgola had said about Kahn's "sense of place." This applies equally to Giurgola's own sense of place.

> For Louis Kahn, place is not a physical entity that can retain a visual image completely. Only the confluence of a human program on the one hand and the natural character of a site on the other eventually produce a place. A place, thus, has an ideology, since it represents a human condition. All the subtle variations of such a condition are contained in it. A place is hardly a statement but, rather, the preparation for one through the careful play between the needs of man and of nature.
>
> Louis Kahn's sense of place . . . stems from an archaic faith, which he consciously asserted in a world little concerned with faith.[2]

It is this faith, the secular spirituality, which both Kahn and Giurgola have been looking for. They both prefer to gently anchor their architecture in the here and now, in the existential situation of the time and the place of its making. Several of Giurgola's projects are testimony to this. But of special interest to me are three of his early projects that were designed during the early 1960s in the Philadelphia studio and which have remained unbuilt. They were conceived at a time when the inadequacies of inherited thought—modernism—were already being sensed but the alternative was not yet clear. Nonetheless, they anticipated much of what followed. All three projects were seeking the nature of an urban place and anchoring their buildings in the physical, cultural and historical context of the city at a time when architecture was preoccupied with making Cartesian objects. Although they remained unbuilt, they predicted much of what Giurgola was able to realize later. I refer to three competition projects, one of which was a winner, but still did not get built, while the other two were placed second.

Major competitions for public buildings are important markers as the judges often represent the prevailing professional establishment. The winning design most likely will reflect the values and concerns of the profession at the time especially if we compare it with the second placed design. This will tell us what has been accepted and what was *consciously* rejected. In a major national competition, there will most likely be an intense deliberation between the first and the second placed schemes. The project placed second will have to be placed there consciously and for good reasons—so one presumes. Thus it will be interesting to look at these three projects against the eventual winners of the competition to explore what may possibly have been the preferred directions of the architectural establishment at that time.

Boston City Hall Competition 1962

The competition for a new City Hall in Boston took place in 1962. The city had decided to clear an entire old part near the historic Faneuil Hall and Quincy Market

(Figure 11.8) to locate this new home for the city government. In the final judgment the entry of Mitchell/Giurgola Architects was placed second. The winning entry by Kallmann McKinnell & Knowles was executed as we see it today (Figure 11.9). At the time of its inauguration, one critic, seemingly knowledgeable about the other entries in the competition, wrote that it "departed from the more conventional designs of most of the other entries—typified by pure geometrical forms clad with sleek curtain walls—to introduce an articulated structure that expressed the internal functions of the buildings in rugged, cantilevered concrete forms."[3]

Figure 11.8
Site of the Boston City Hall before demolition. Faneuil Hall can be seen in the background.

Figure 11.9
Boston City Hall. Kallmann McKinnell & Knowles, Boston, MA, USA, 1963.

Interestingly, this description can also apply to the second placed scheme of Mitchell/Giurgola Architects, indicating that the two entries may have been very close in the jury discussion in terms of their architectonic qualities. The difference, then, lies in their respective sense of the public place and its relation with the city. A look at Giurgola's site plan makes this clear (Figure 11.10). The U-shaped office structure and the semi-detached Council building together establish a series of public places connecting the center of the new building and the front of the Council Chamber with the historic Faneuil Hall and the Quincy Market (Figure 11.11) with a pedestrian plaza bridging over the road on the east of the site (Figure 11.12). The Council Chamber, supposedly the heart of the city government, is thus directly connected with Faneuil Hall, referred to as the "Cradle of American Freedom." Describing this, Giurgola wrote:

> at its core, a major space, without romantic configurations or mysteries, that is a symbolic replacement of the traditional front door of the city hall [Figure 11.13]. Open and unforbidding, this square, by providing simple, single-level continuity between it and the public offices surrounding it, is an expression of the new approachability of the city government . . . the offices are not allowed to dominate the ceremonial space, however. The council building is placed in direct relation to Faneuil Hall and Dock Square (Quincy Market) linking the old with the new, the large with the small.[4]

What distinguishes this proposal from the eventual winner, then, is not their respective architectonic choices but their respective sense of history, sense of the city and the quality of the public place infused with secular spirituality at the birthplace of American democracy. The tension created between the monumentality of architecture on the one hand and the subtle place making on the other leads to an ambiguity, together with the contextual sensitivity, that is unfamiliar to the orthodox modernist discourse in architecture.

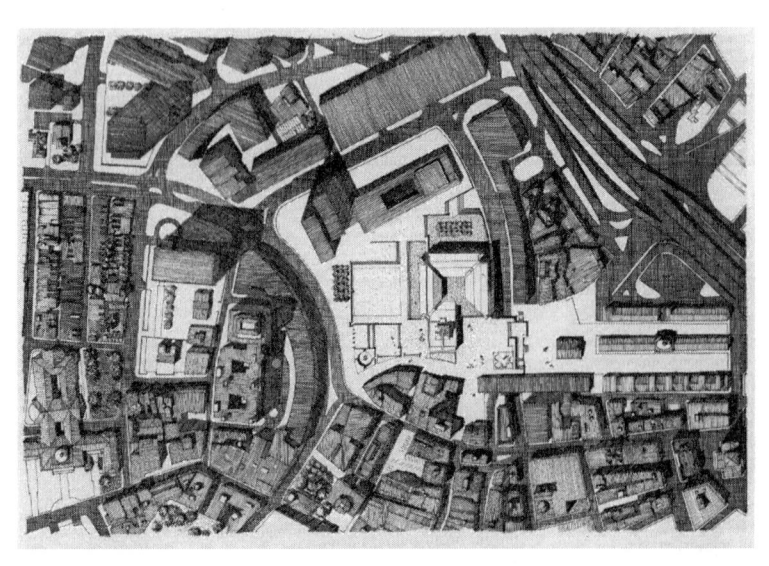

Figure 11.10 **Proposed site plan. Mitchell/ Giurgola Architects, Boston City Hall Competition proposal, Boston, MA, USA, 1962. Notice the connection with the Faneuil Hall and Quincy Market.**

Figure 11.11
**Site model,
Boston City
Hall project.
Mitchell/
Giurgola
Architects,
Boston, MA,
USA, 1962.**

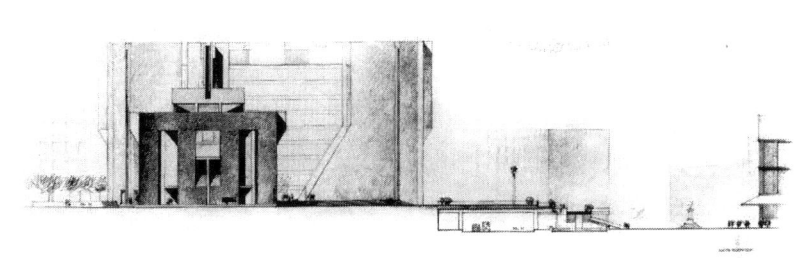

Figure 11.12
**Sketch showing
relationship of
the proposal
with the Faneuil
Hall. Mitchell/
Giurgola
Architects,
Boston, MA,
USA, 1962.**

Figure 11.13
**Sketch by
Giurgola. Notice
the spatial
continuity
between the
plaza and the
entrance square.
Mitchell/
Giurgola
Architects,
Boston, MA,
USA, 1962.**

International House Competition 1965

Situated near the University of Pennsylvania campus the brief called for housing for an international community of 432 students. The difference between Mitchell/Giurgola's design, placed second, and that of the eventual winner, designed by the local firm of Bower & Fradley Architects, cannot be more emphatic (Figures 11.14 and 11.15). Departing from the prevailing modernist strategies, Giurgola went back to his experience of early European urbanism to evolve the plan form for this building. In a typical pre-modern European city both the edges of the site and the extent of the building coincide. Architecture thus defines both the regular and the ideal fields controlling all spaces within the site, without leaving any residual spaces. At the aggregate level of the city, buildings occupy their respective sites all the way up to the edge, leaving only that which is public domain—either a street or a square.

Interestingly, this phenomenon is found not only in Europe but also in most pre-modern, pre-rationalist cultures and indicates an alternative conception of space, and a relationship between the public and private realms in cities. Take the beautiful inlay pattern from Alhambra shown in Figure 11.16. It shows a "triangular" form in various shades on a white background. However, if you focus on the shapes of the white gaps left, you will realize that they are the same as the brown and blue shapes (shown in grey and black here). In other words, the

Figure 11.14
International House as built. Bower & Fradley Architects, Philadelphia, USA, 1970.

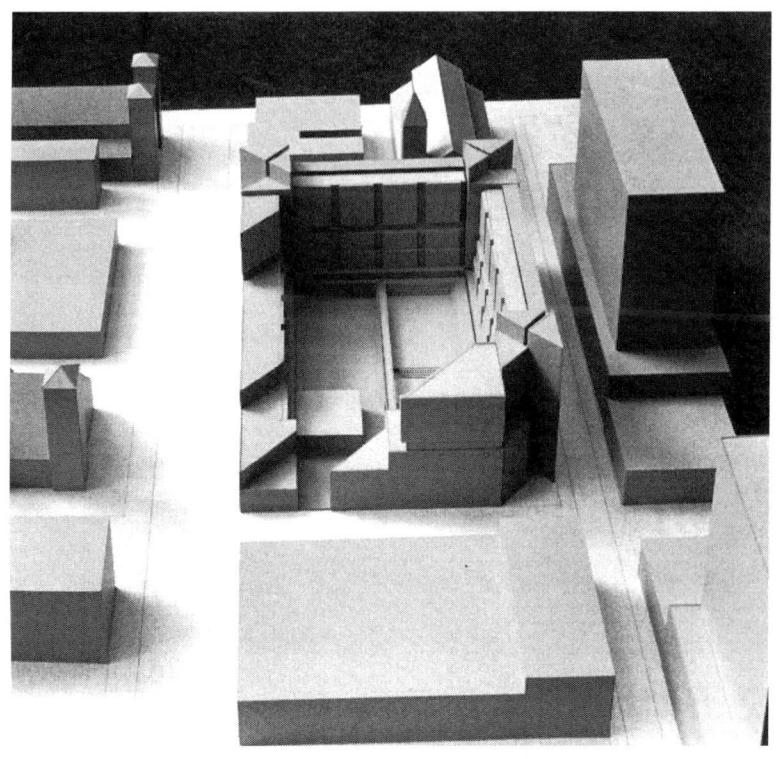

Figure 11.15
**Model of
Mitchell/
Giurgola's
proposal for the
International
House. Mitchell/
Giurgola
Architects,
International
House
Competition
proposal,
Philadelphia,
USA, 1965.**

ground is as "figural" as the figure. Extend this to the city and it tells you that a building is complete only to the extent it completes the public space.

Such a relationship between the building (figure) and the public space (ground) is evident in Giurgola's design for the International House. It begins with the initial decision to occupy the entire site and thereby establish a positive dialog with the neighboring buildings (Figure 11.17). In doing this Giurgola recognizes and acknowledges the urban character of Philadelphia blocks. Several

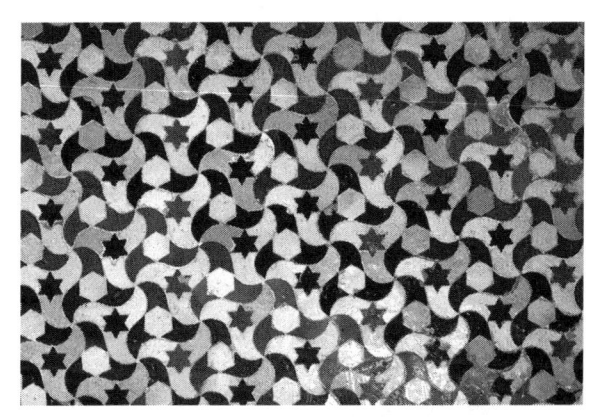

Figure 11.16
**Inlay pattern,
bath house
at Alhambra
Palace, Granada,
Spain. Notice
the similarity
between the
figure and the
ground.**

consequences follow from this initial decision. First, the courtyard now emerges as a positive space—a room without a roof—for outdoor gatherings of the young occupants. Second, this courtyard is deliberately oriented diagonally toward the university campus at the south-east by careful modulation of the architecture of the wings facing Chestnut and 37th Streets (Figure 11.18). And third, the residential suites facing the courtyard are expressed in the language of repeatable openings[5] while the public spaces facing the streets are expressed through large openings in response to the scale of the city (Figures 11.19 and 11.20).

Figure 11.17
Plan of the International House proposal. Mitchell/ Giurgola Architects, Philadelphia, USA, 1965.

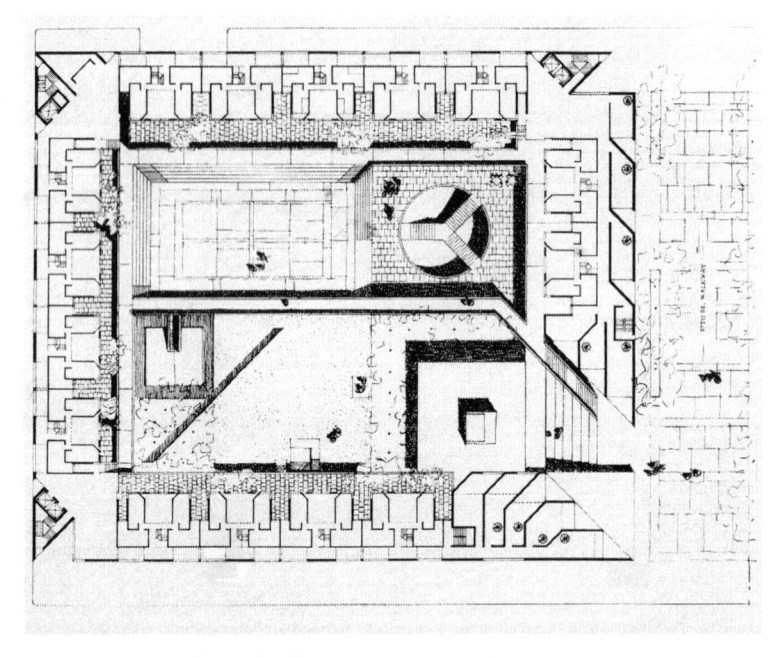

Figure 11.18
Model. Notice the open corner orienting the building toward the university. Mitchell/ Giurgola Architects, International House Competition proposal, Philadelphia, USA, 1965.

Figure 11.19
Sketch of the courtyard, International House. Romaldo Giurgola, Philadelphia, USA, 1965.

Figure 11.20
Part elevation of the residential suites facing the courtyard, International House. Romaldo Giurgola, Philadelphia, USA, 1965.

All this gives this building a high degree of specificity. It is firmly located in its specific address; it cannot be moved to any other place and remain the same. This is precisely what Giurgola had said about Kahn's sense of place: "Only the confluence of a human program on the one hand and the natural character of a site on the other eventually produce a place. A place, thus, has an ideology, since it represents a human condition."

This building, then, embodies multiple narratives each of which—urbanism, the sense of place and the existential specificity of architecture—raises questions about the normative architectural practices of the last 200 years; modernism had taken very different approaches on all these matters. We have no idea about the jury or its deliberations while arriving at the final decision. The winning entry has produced an elegant building and it cannot be faulted as an aesthetic object. But seeing both these designs together makes it clear that in 1965 the questions raised by Giurgola's design not only distinguished it from the eventual winner but also constituted a critique of the prevailing modernist conventions. True, there already was a growing uneasiness towards modernism but this uneasiness with the prevailing architectural thought was not yet wholeheartedly articulated and accepted, and Giurgola's project, though not realized, remains an important marker for having pushed the boundaries a little further.

National Headquarters Building, AIA, 1965

Mitchell/Giurgola's submission in the national design competition was the winning entry from among 221 contestants. And yet it did not get built and became one of the most disappointing chapters in the life of the firm. Located on an irregularly shaped site at the junction of New York Avenue and 18th Street in Washington DC, the plot contains the Octagon House, the third most historic building in the US capital (Figure 11.21). The competition brief had specifically asked for the new building to "preserve, complement and enhance the historic residence" and for it to be "an exciting demonstration that fresh and contemporary architecture can live in harmony with fine architecture of another period; each statement giving the other more meaning and contributing to the delight of the entire building complex."[6] Describing the original scheme (Figures 11.22, 11.23 and 11.24) (the design went through several modifications before Mitchell/Giurgola resigned the commission), Giurgola wrote:

> The building order develops naturally from the conditions of the site, orienting toward the garden and facing the Octagon: the building form completed only by its presence. The great curved glass wall acts as a foil, complementing the Octagon. The garden is a quiet place to stay, a meeting ground of the historically traditional and the contemporary.[7]

The most significant sentence in the above statement refers to the inseparable reciprocity between the new building and the Octagon House: "the building form completed only by its presence." The logic of the new design thus presupposes the presence of the old building: it is incomplete without the Octagon.

This, then, is the primary narrative of this design: the mutual recognition and interdependence between the old and the new, one mirroring the other. The place created in between the two is thus impregnated with the secular spirituality which has less to do with the shape of the new building or its internal arrangements. In the process the Octagon House is invested with a new meaning. Built in 1800 for a plantation owner and designed by Dr. William Thornton, the architect of the US Capitol Building, it had served as a temporary home for President Madison. Since 1899 it had become home for the American Institute

Figure 11.21
The Octagon House. William Thornton, Washington, DC, 1801.

Figure 11.22
Model showing the relationship between the curved glass wall and the Octagon. Mitchell/ Giurgola Architects, AIA Headquarters Competition proposal, Washington, DC, 1965.

of Architects. Now it is called upon to partner a twentieth-century building in creating a unique public place in the city of Washington (Figure 11.25). It is the architecture of this *place* that is central to Giurgola's design. It recognizes history,

Figure 11.23
**Model of
the winning
proposal
for the AIA
Headquarters
building.
Mitchell/
Giurgola
Architects, AIA
Headquarters
Competition
proposal,
Washington,
DC, 1965.**

Figure 11.24
**Plan of the
winning
proposal. AIA
Headquarters
building.
Mitchell/
Giurgola
Architects,
Washington,
DC, 1965.**

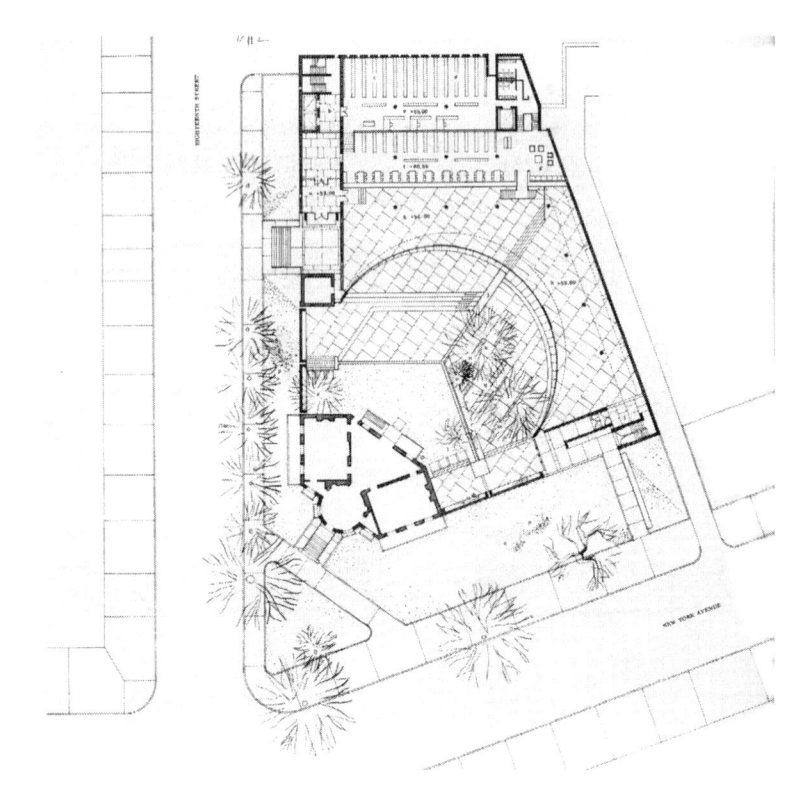

gains something from it and gives it back a new layer of meaning. Giurgola has thus located himself firmly in the historical process and created a place full of reverence for the city and humankind.

After announcing the result of the competition, the program was expanded and more land was acquired from the adjoining plot. Mitchell/Giurgola was asked to modify the design to accommodate new conditions. The new design accommodated the expanded program without compromising the core values (Figures 11.26 and 11.27). At this point, the regulations required that every building in Washington's historic area be cleared by a review board, the Fine Arts Commission. Unfortunately, the Commission had strong views about the Octagon House and felt that the new building should be only a quiet backdrop to this historic structure. One of the prominent members of the Commission was Gordon Bunshaft, a senior partner in the firm of Skidmore, Owings & Merrill (SOM). He led the view of the Commission that the proposed new building was inappropriate for this site. It is interesting to note here that while the official architectural establishment, in the form of the American Institute of Architects, the client body which had organized the competition, had already accepted and welcomed the new ideas and values embodied in Giurgola's design, there was still a powerful group of individuals who still resisted this and for whom Octagon was a pristine object to be preserved and celebrated only with a quiet and neutral background.

Between 1965 and 1968 Mitchell/Giurgola produced more than half a dozen variations of their design to save the project but none could satisfy the Fine Arts Commission. Their final scheme came closest to what the Commission wanted but not quite close enough (Figures 11.28 and 11.29). Finally in September of

Figure 11.25
Sketch of the interior looking out toward the back of Octagon, AIA Headquarters building. Romaldo Giurgola, Philadelphia, 1965.

Figure 11.26
Model. Revised proposal, AIA Headquarters building. Mitchell/ Giurgola Architects, Washington, DC, 1965.

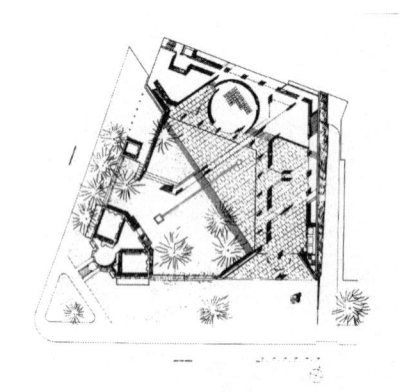

Figure 11.27
Plan. Revised proposal, AIA Headquarters building. Mitchell/ Giurgola Architects, Washington, DC, 1965.

1968, Mitchell/Giurgola resigned. The President of the AIA, George E. Kassabaum, is reported to have said that "the differences between the architect and the Commission were irreconcilable: What the Commission found unacceptable, the architect considered critical to his design concept."[8] What was so critical for Giurgola? We may get a hint of it if we look at what was finally built on the site.

The project was finally awarded to The Architects Collaborative (TAC), the firm founded by Walter Gropius in 1946. Its design was executed and occupied in 1973 (Figure 11.30). Again, if taken by itself and under the circumstances in which it came about, what the city of Washington finally got is not bad. It is well crafted and sits quietly behind the Octagon but without engaging with it in the way Giurgola had envisioned, and thereby keeping it as an abstract object in the

Figure 11.28
Model. Final attempt at reconciliation, AIA Headquarters building. Mitchell/ Giurgola Architects, Washington, DC, 1965.

Figure 11.29
Sketch of the final proposal, AIA Headquarters building. Mitchell/ Giurgola Architects, Washington, DC, 1965.

true modernist orthodoxy. Giurgola would have none of this. His contact with architecture was made in the here and now and not in timeless and placeless abstractions. Octagon was, for him, a real presence to engage with and only in such a condition is the place between the two buildings impregnated with meaning and spirituality that transcend the formal qualities or the historicity of

Figure 11.30
AIA Headquarters building as built, in relation to the Octagon House. The Architects Collaborative, Washington, DC, 1973.

either of the buildings. But for that to happen, the prevailing establishment had to be receptive to a different set of values. This was just beginning to happen.[9] In his announcement of Mitchell/Giurgola's resignation, President George E. Kassabaum, FAIA emphasized that, while the AIA continued to support the principle of design review, in this instance it disagreed with the Commission's ruling.[10]

Clearly, this points to a simultaneous co-existence of two approaches to architecture not fully compatible with each other. One, representing the modernist orthodoxy, favored clean, sleek and straight-forward geometric abstractions; the other celebrated subtleties and location-specific, humanly scaled and accommodating place making. The former represented the professional establishment, raised and conditioned by 300 years of modernist history, while the latter, representing the younger generation of architects and critics, posed a serious critique of the orthodoxy through their work. Commenting on the above events, one critic later wrote:

> Ironically enough, the same course of events probably would not occur today in the same way. For the architectural biases have been realigned in their influence. Whereas the Mitchell/Giurgola approach was then so new, difficult, and without a strong platform, the SOM brand of architecture had reached its heyday in public and professional appeal and acceptance . . . Today, the tables haven't turned but they are tipping in Giurgola's direction.[11]

All three of these projects represent a stage in Giurgola's career when he was emerging as an independent force in his own right. Later in his career, he was able to bring to fruition all the above concerns to a finely tuned resolution in many realized projects. The relationship with Louis Kahn remained at a much deeper level whereby both were engaged in critiquing, in their own way, the received wisdom of the modern movement. Few works of architecture from the second half of the twentieth century have been more influential and have marked so fundamental a paradigm shift in the modern movement in architecture as Kahn's Richards Medical Research building and the Trenton Jewish Community Center and Bath House. The categories of "servant" and "served" spaces, which these two buildings contributed to the architectural discourse, as well as a new formal vocabulary, implied a fundamental departure from the modernist conventions. All three Giurgola projects—Boston City Hall, the International House and the AIA Headquarters—were contemporary to these works of Kahn. Seen in the context of their respective relationship with history, urbanism and sense of place, it becomes evident that their paths crossed but also diverged, as it should be.

Notes

1　Romaldo Giurgola and Jaimini Mehta, *Louis I. Kahn, Architect* (Boulder: Westview Press, 1975), 244.
2　Ibid., 57–58.
3　*Wikipedia*, "Boston City Hall," available at: https://en.wikipedia.org/wiki/Boston_City_Hall.
4　Romaldo Giurgola, *Boston City Hall Competition Report.* Competition brief (Boston: Mitchell/Giurgola Asso. Architects, 1962).
5　Giurgola himself has described this courtyard as "a parade of houses in a square, like in a city, facing toward the University."
6　Quoted by Ada Louise Huxtable, *The New York Times*, Sunday July 12, 1970.
7　Giurgola's note with the competition entry.
8　*Washington Post*, "Architects' Own Office Plan Rejected," *Washington Post* (Sept. 24, 1968).
9　It is interesting to note that the term "contextualism" entered modern architectural lexicon only around the 1970s.
10　Max O. Urbahn, "Evolution of the Octagon Building," *AIA Journal* (June 1973), 50.
11　Suzanne Stephens, "A.I.A. HQ: Magnificent Intentions," *Architectural Forum*, 140(3) (Oct. 1973), 42.

Chapter 12

The Vienna Spring

It can be argued that modern design in general, and architecture in particular, arrived at its stylistic peak and consistency in turn-of-the-century Vienna. The *Wiener Moderne* movement between 1890 and 1918, also known as the Vienna Secessionist movement, was propelled by the growing awareness that the then prevailing forms of expressions in art, architecture, music and also urbanism, still directed by the academic traditions, no longer corresponded with the emerging patterns of social life and needed to change. This led to an unusual congruence of ideas and arts made possible by the simultaneous presence of minds like Sigmund Freud, Ludwig Wittgenstein, Gustav Mahler, Arnold Schoenberg, Gustav Klimt, Otto Wagner, Josef Hoffmann, Adolf Loos and many others. This intellectual hyperactivity had the potential to fulfill the promises contained in the original idea of modernity: the rational organization of the day-to-day life of the society and its expression in visual arts, architecture and music. What this group of thinkers and artists produced in three decades still dazzle us. Unfortunately, this creative experiment was disrupted and then derailed by the hostilities that engulfed Europe in 1914–1918.

Two characteristics define this movement. One, its extraordinary ability to co-populate, in an art object, both the emotional and the rational realities. And this had something to do with the second characteristic, that is, the social recognition of the autonomous individual and subsequently the emergence of an artist with the freedom to freely express reality as they see it. In the context of Vienna at the turn of the twentieth century, this duality of the emotional and rational corresponded with the internal and external realities of the individual. Sigmund Freud's investigations had uncovered hidden structures of thought and emotions and brought them to the surface. This confronted Viennese society with a peculiar situation: up to this time, the society in Vienna, including the new aristocracy and the bourgeoisie who supported avant-garde art, had structured itself in terms of the separation of the private and the public spheres; a person's private thoughts and emotions were not for public expression. This guaranteed equilibrium, order and appropriate communication between and across various segments of the society. The emergence of the autonomous individual[1] and the breach of strict separation between the private and the public, between the emotional and rational, placed the private on a par with the public and gave individual emotions a public dimension so far hidden behind a public order. Art was supposed to be the visual expression of this public order with exact canons laid down about what was presentable in public. It was this that the Secessionist movement aimed to secede from. Not surprisingly, many of the leading figures of this movement, including Freud, Schoenberg and Hoffmann, came under constant criticism though artists such as Gustav Klimt (painting), Grete Wiesenthal (dance) and Arnold Schoenberg (music) were able to push the limits of expression with bright color, free movement and atonality.

Otto Wagner's Postal Savings Bank, completed in 1906 (Figure 12.1), is a good example of a functional building dedicated to monetary transactions, acquiring a transcendental quality through architectural choices and detailing. The façade, unlike that of the neighboring buildings, is clad in thin marble panels (Figure 12.2). This is clearly a case of embracing the new construction technology and its rationale is laid out in the architect's own notes:

> The façade . . . is to be . . . clad in panels. The projected cubage of these panels can be relatively small, but the projected material should be of high quality (such as Laas marble) . . . The result . . . will be approximately the following: The stone cubages will be reduced from 1/10 to 1/50 . . . The monumental effect will be enhanced by the precious material, the costs will be massively reduced and the construction time will be brought down to the short period desired.[2]

A rational decision indeed but Wagner wanted to go beyond; though these panels are fixed to the base wall with mortar, they are also bolted and the bolts are expressed, with aluminum button caps, as the new ornament (Figure 12.3)—ornamentation that has emerged out of the nature of construction. The façade is

Figure 12.1
Main façade seen from Georg-Coch Platz. Otto Wagner, Postal Savings Bank, Vienna, Austria, 1905.

enriched by the narrative of its making; the building tells the story of how it was made. Wagner not only departed from the established past conventions of public architecture but also in the process introduced a new idea of ornamentation, which clearly had emotional validity, derived from the construction process itself.

The choice of darker material and the pronounced horizontal lines in the base of the building respond to the prevailing grammar in the immediately surrounding buildings and maintain the existing urban order. The reassertion of the vertical in the corner sections on either side of the entrance is an indication that the façade is a delicate balancing act between conflicting pulls.

Compared to Wagner's urban bank building with its large mass, Josef Hoffmann's Palais Stoclet is a relatively modest residence in Brussels. Viewed from the street, it presents itself as a simple, unadorned but dignified and stately mansion with its plain façade clad in stone slabs (Figure 12.4). On closer inspection, however, it reveals the complex corporeal massing and spatial form.

Figure 12.2
Detail view near entrance. Otto Wagner, Postal Savings Bank, Vienna, Austria, 1905.

Figure 12.3
Detail of marble panels and the aluminum button caps. Otto Wagner, Postal Savings Bank, Vienna, Austria, 1905.

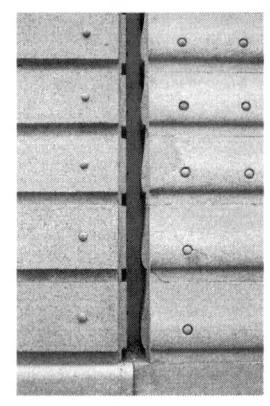

The seemingly articulated mass of the building is held together by the central three-storeyed rectangular element with pitched roof. Several secondary elements are attached to this central mass on all four sides and also on part of the roof (Figure 12.5). However, this articulation of mass is not reflected in the spatial organization and is also not obvious from the outside.

One of these attached elements is the entrance pavilion which stretches out from the façade up to the edge of the site on the street side. This is the axis of approach and relates the house to the public realm of the city (Figure 12.6). There is another, more formal, axis, parallel to the former, which relates the

Figure 12.4
View from Avenue Tervueren. Josef Hoffmann, Palais Stoclet, Brussels, Belgium, 1905.

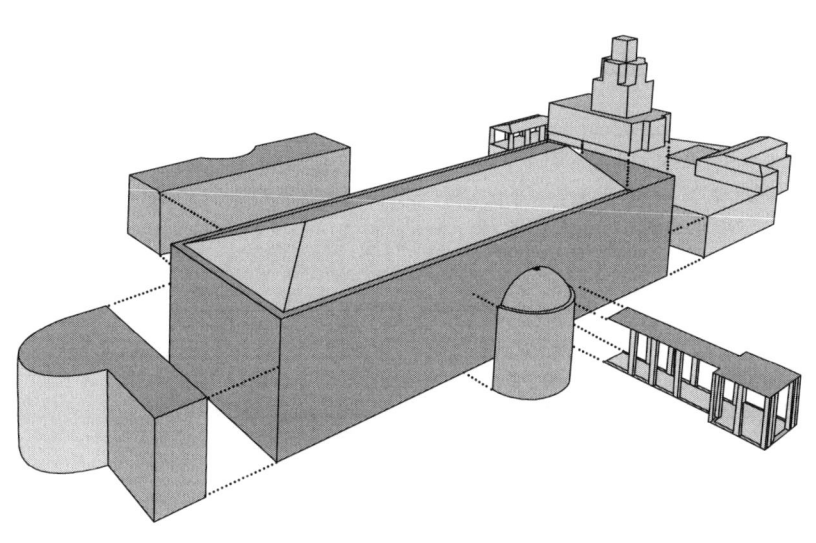

Figure 12.5
Volumetric analysis of the corporeal form. Josef Hoffmann, Palais Stoclet, Brussels, Belgium, 1905.

social core of the house to the private realm of the garden. Except for these two exes, geometry has very little role to play in revealing the spatial order of this remarkable building. This order is revealed through perception and not geometry; one has to bodily move through the complex set of connections between various spaces, with all their senses alert, to realize that it is an experiential space requiring our sensuous engagement. For example, even though the dining room and the study/smoking room are both symmetrically positioned on either side of the formal axis facing the garden, suggesting their parity, we become aware of another parity between the music room and the dining room only when we

Figure 12.6
Floor plan. Ground floor shows the primary axial structure. Josef Hoffmann, Palais Stoclet, Brussels, Belgium, 1905.

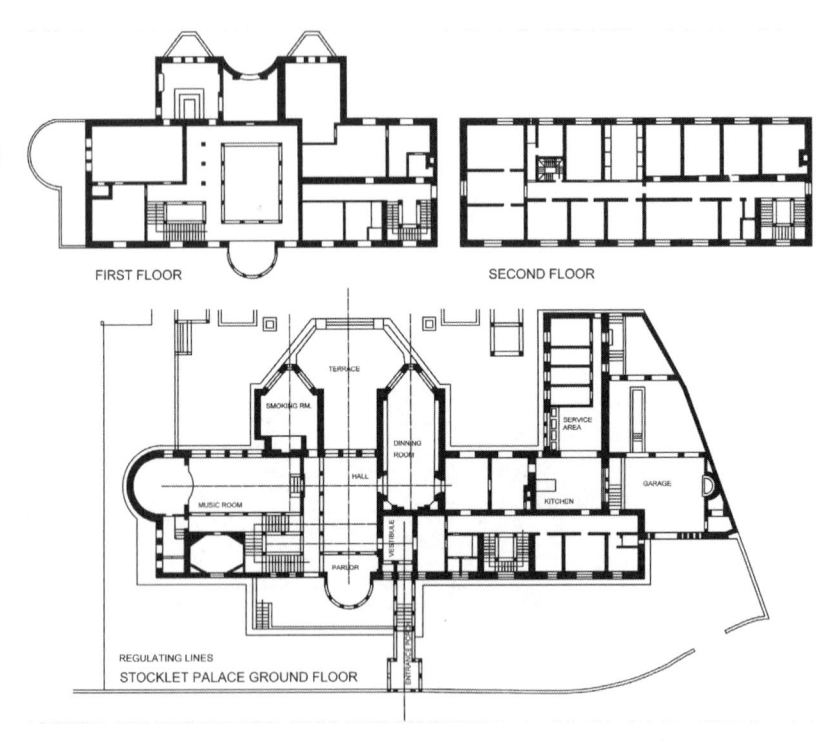

Figure 12.7
Interior view. Josef Hoffmann, Palais Stoclet, Brussels, Belgium, 1905.

locate ourselves at the exact point where the line connecting their respective doors crosses the formal axis. Similarly, even the stair leading to the upper floor is not so obvious but has to be "discovered" by actually moving about the hall (Figure 12.7). The space is indeed structured and, in that respect, there is rationality albeit moderated by perception. The space is co-made by our bodily movement. Architecture is contingent upon occupation.

The treatment of exterior corners throughout this building has been an enigma. Hoffmann has deliberately highlighted these with dark-colored tubular stone (Figure 12.8). We do not know the architect's intention behind this unusual detail: Hoffmann has not left any notes of his deliberations. We can only advance a conjecture based on our perception. Drawing our attention to the outlines of the form does question the solidity of the mass and the materiality of its surfaces. This is like a shape indicated by its wire-frame form: we do not know if it is solid or void. Was Hoffmann presenting an ambiguity or subconsciously anticipating the onset of a new space conception which, only a few years later his younger colleagues, Walter Gropius and Mies van der Rohe, were able to express so successfully, with the use of glass and steel frames?

The Vienna Secessionist group embraced the idea of total design and, in addition to architecture, also produced furniture design (Figure 12.9), glass, ceramic and metalware (Figure 12.10), painting, textile design and even music and dance. Its ambition was no less than to touch all walks of life and transform and modernize them thoroughly. Arnold Schoenberg challenged classical music's compositional tradition of using eight tonal notes and developed a method of manipulating all twelve notes of the chromatic scale. This gave freedom to individual composers to improvise and develop variations without having to follow an overarching central idea. "The emancipation of the dissonance" is how he described his music with its free floating atonality.

Figure 12.8
All corners highlighted by darker material. Josef Hoffmann, Palais Stoclet, Brussels, Belgium, 1905.

Figure 12.9
"Cafe Museum Chair," Adolf Loos, an example of the Weiner Werkstatte design, Vienna, Austria, 1911.

Grete Wiesenthal was inspired by the American dancer Isadora Duncan's tours of Europe around 1900. Her form of dance was inspired more by intuition than a predetermined structure: "One movement gives birth to the next" is how she is reported to have described her dance (Figure 12.11). The new sense of female freedom this brought in led to a shift away from the classical ballet and towards free expressive dance.

This break from the past was far more radical than could be explained by the Hegelian terms of thesis, antithesis and synthesis. The two buildings analyzed above, Otto Wagner's Postal Savings Bank and Josef Hoffmann's Palais Stoclet, as well as the other developments in art, music and dance, demonstrate that this extraordinary flowering of art and design in Vienna is yet to be fully understood. For example, what followed after the war was not

Figure 12.10
Porcelain tea and coffeeware, Jutta Sika, an example of the Weiner Werkstatte design, Vienna, Austria, 1901–1902.

Figure 12.11
Grete Wiesenthal in one of her performances.

a variation or continuation of the Vienna movement but markedly different in its understanding of the relationship between humans and technology and the purpose of art. In this respect, the Viennese group was closer to William Morris and Charles Rennie Mackintosh. One is tempted to ask, why did the Deutscher Werkbund, younger sibling of the Weiner Werkstatte (Viennese Workshop) and precursor to the Bauhaus, gain currency after the war while the latter had to be closed down? That too was inspired by the Arts and Crafts movement.

The answer may be found if we broaden our inquiry. Though the emergence of the Vienna Spring may be attributed to the presence of a number of extraordinary artists and thinkers, its premature end may not have been caused by only the political upheaval of the First World War and the fragmentation of the Austro-Hungarian empire; its eventual demise may have been built into the very nature of the movement itself. Both the two characteristics I mentioned earlier, namely the coming together of the emotional and the rational, or the private and the public, and the emergence of the autonomous individual, proved to be difficult to sustain, in the same spirit as in Vienna, with increasing industrialization. Even with their beautifully expressive metalwork, glassware and furniture designs, the Viennese designers were not thinking of industrial mass production. In fact, one of first critical assessments of Wiener Werkstatte's work in 1904 observed:

> Every object thus embodies technical and spiritual endeavour to the highest degree, and its artistic worth resides where it is seldom found and should in very truth be sought: not solely in decorative externals and formalistic trimmings, but rather in the seriousness and dignity of mental and manual labour.[3]

Compare this with the fact that in Germany a similar organization, the Deutscher Werkbund, was formed in 1907 by Herman Muthesius to harness the potential of mass production to make German industry more globally competitive. Similarly, Otto Wagner's observation that "the architect always has to develop the art-form out of *construction*"[4] (italics mine) was referring to the craft of construction, the art of carefully putting together a building, while the rest of Europe was preparing to celebrate the abstract idea of technology through standardization. Functionalism had by then acquired the stature of a gospel. Adolf Loos, Wagner's pupil, had already equated ornament with crime in 1910 and thereby added a moral dimension to architecture and design. This suggests that the contradictions were only just below the surface and may even be deep-rooted.

The challenge that the Vienna Succession movement posed was not only to the prevailing aristocracy, or to the separation of the public and the private spheres of life but to the very foundation on which the edifice of modernism and capitalism was to be built: the Kantian separation of mind and body and the primacy accorded to the rational mind. We can locate a potential contradiction here: the individual, liberated by modernity, was not just a rational mind but "the concrete human being with all his emotional, intellectual, and sensuous potentialities."[5] Being an autonomous individual is a far more difficult and complex phenomenon than it appears to be. Referring to individuation, Erich Fromm makes an important point that it is not enough to be freed *from* the traditional patterns of behavior imposed by society; one should also be able to exercise freedom *to* think and act for oneself in order to be truly autonomous. This is the real sense in which autonomy implied freedom but this is not an easy state of being and how one deals with it often depends upon the belief system and spiritual upbringing that shapes our sense of self. Giving an example, Fromm writes, "This development had been prepared by the teachings of the Reformation . . . Protestantism made the individual face God alone." He goes on to say, "the affirmation of the individual which capitalism brought about, it also led to a self-negation and asceticism which is the direct continuation of the Protestant spirit."[6]

Self-negation and asceticism were farthest from the minds of the Vienna artists and this is reflected in the exuberance of their work. But then it may have something to do with the fact that many of them, and their patrons, were Jewish, and though they were assimilated in the largely Catholic Austro-Hungarian society (anti-Semitism had not yet raised its ugly head), their response to the oncoming winds of change may have been shaped by their individual psychological and emotional make-up. Popular Judaism, with its mystic and Kabbalistic traditions, may have already prepared its followers for the mystical/experiential orientation of the Vienna artists.[7] My own familiarity with Jewish metaphysics is at best superfluous but a few friends have enlightened me that in the Kabbalah tradition both intuition and understanding are referred to by the single term, *Binah*, which is placed high in the hierarchy of qualities, on a par with *Chokmah*, which is intellect that does not emanate from rational process. Looking back at his memoirs on the Vienna of his youth, Oskar Kokoschka recalled:

> Most of my sitters were Jews. They felt less secure than the rest of the Viennese Establishment, and were consequently more open to the new and more sensitive to the tensions and pressures that accompanied the decay of the old order in Austria.[8]

Clearly, not everyone responded to individuation in a similar way. Still, there was a significant number of artists and thinkers in Vienna during that time who not only benefited from the freedom *from* the old order but were also able to exercise this new freedom *to* think for themselves and simultaneously occupy in their work the dual worlds of reason and emotion, cerebral and experiential, all at once.

But it is this—the co-existence of the rational and the non-rational—that was precisely what was becoming increasingly difficult in a world determined to align day-to-day life, including art, with science and technology. The process had begun soon after the war. The Bauhaus was already showing signs of inner contradictions. For example, inspired by the English Arts and Crafts movement, many of its founders were themselves practicing architects and hands-on artists. In April 1919, Gropius wrote, we must all return to the crafts! For there is no "professional art." Artists are craftsmen in the original sense of the word, and only in rare, blessed moments of revelation that lie outside the power of their will can art blossom unconsciously from the work of their hands.[9]

He reiterated this in the founding manifesto of Bauhaus, "The artist is an exalted craftsman." On the other hand, only a few years later, in the "unofficial" manifesto of Bauhaus of 1923 Oskar Schlemmer wrote,

reason and science, "man's greatest powers" are the regents, and the engineer is the sedate executor of unlimited possibilities. Mathematics, structure, and mechanization are the elements, and power and money are the dictators of these modern phenomena of steel, concrete, glass and electricity.[10]

And in 1928 Hannes Meyer, who succeeded Gropius as head of the Bauhaus echoed these sentiments when he presented his programs to the students:

- All things in this world are a product of the formula: (function times economy).
- All these things are, therefore, not works of art: all art is composition and hence, is unsuited to achieve goals.
- All life is function and is therefore unartistic.[11]

The Bauhaus was closed in 1933 under pressure from the Nazi regime but one of its students, Max Bill, opened the Hochschule für Gestaltung (HfG) at Ulm on similar academic principles in 1953. For a while Bill continued the Bauhaus approach that still considered the artist-designer as the individual "author" of their work. But academism had already taken hold of the school and in 1956 Bill was replaced by Tomas Maldonado. From then onward, analytical methods, operational science and systems-thinking became the preferred approaches.

That both Bauhaus and HfG-Ulm produced excellent designs and architecture is beyond dispute. Still, it is difficult to see both as the logical continuation of the Vienna Spring. Both Vienna and Bauhaus–Ulm were informed by different sets of ideas. The metaphysical foundations of the latter were already laid two centuries ago when the rational mind was prioritized over the senses and experience. Starting with Laugier, who pointed a finger at the rustic hut, the architectural intelligentsia was prolific in preparing the ground for this. The rationalism inherent in the writings of Eugène Viollet-le-Duc, Henri Labrouste and Auguste Choisy, and the functionalism of the twentieth century had all made it inevitable. In that respect the Vienna Secessionist movement can be seen as an aberration, albeit a beautiful one, in this larger historical narrative.

But comparisons can be misleading. We do not want to compare the Vienna Spring with Bauhaus-Ulm to uncover their relative values; this is irrelevant. What is important is to see each as a foil against which the other can be clearly articulated. Seen this way, Vienna offers a powerful critique of the modern movement in architecture as we have come to recognize it.

Notes

1   Erich Fromm, *Escape From Freedom* (New York: Avon Books, 1967).
2   Quoted in Federal Press Service, *Vienna Modernism, 1890–1910* (Vienna: Federal Press Service, 1999), 36.
3   Joseph August Lux, quoted by Amanda Dunsmore in *Vienna Art and Design*, exhibition catalogue (Melbourne, National Gallery of Victoria. 2011), 170.
4   Quoted by Christian Witt-Dorring in *Vienna: Art and Design*, ibid., 6.
5   Erich Fromm, ibid., 130.
6   Ibid., 128–130.
7   Gershom Scholem, *Major Trends in Jewish Mysticism* (New York: Schocken Books, 1974).
8   Edward Timms, "The Golden Ages of Jewish Austro-Hungary," *Times Literary Supplement* (Feb. 20, 2013).
9   Ulrich Conrads, *Programs and Manifestoes on 20th-Century Architecture* (Cambridge, MA: MIT Press, 1970), 46.
10 Ibid., 70.
11 Ibid., 117.

Bibliography

Acharya, Pransanna Kumar, ed. and trans., *Architecture of Mansara* (Delhi: Low Price Publications, 2006).

Alberti, Leone Batista, *The Ten Books of Architecture*, trans. James Leoni, ed. Joseph Rykwert (London: Alec Tiranti, 1965).

Arendt, Hannah, *The Human Condition* (Chicago: University of Chicago, 1958).

Banham, Reyner, *Theory and Design in the First Machine Age* (New York: Praeger, 1972).

Bell, Daniel, *The End of Ideology* (New York: The Free Press, 1965).

Benjamin, Walter, "Paris: Capital of the Nineteenth Century," *Perspecta*, 12 (1969), 163–172.

Bertalanffy, Ludwig von, *General System Theory* (New York: George Braziller, 1968).

Bohm, David, *Wholeness and the Implicate Order* (London: Ark Paperbacks, 1983).

Carlo, Giancarlo De, "Legitimizing Architecture," *Forum*, 23(1) (1972), 8–20.

Carlyle, Thomas, *The French Revolution: A History* (London: Chapman & Hall, 1896).

Cassirer, Ernst, *The Philosophy of Symbolic Forms*, vol. 2 (New Haven: Yale University Press, 1968).

Chakrabarti, Arindam, "Rationality in Indian Philosophy." In *A Companion to World Philosophies*, ed. E. Deutsch and R. Bontekoe (Oxford, 1991), 259–278.

Conrads, Ulrich, *Programs and Manifestos in 20th-Century Architecture* (Cambridge, MA: MIT Press, 1970).

Correa, Charles, "Transfers and Transformations." In *Charles Correa* (Singapore: Concept Media Ltd., 1987), 165–175.

Dagens, Bruno, trans., *Mayamatam Treatise on Housing, Architecture and Iconography* (New Delhi, Motilal Banarasidas Publishers, 1994).

David Bohm and Hiley, Basil J., *The Undivided Universe: An Ontological Interpretation of Quantum Theory* (New York: Routledge, 1993).

Diebold, John T., *Automation: The Advent of the Automatic Factory* (Princeton: Van Nostrand, 1952).

Eisenman, Peter, "The Debate: Contrasting Concepts of Harmony in Architecture," *Lotus International*, 40 (1983), 60–68.

Federal Press Service, *Vienna Modernism 1890–1910* (Vienna: Federal Press Service, 1999).

Frampton, Kenneth, *Modern Architecture: A Critical History* (New York: Oxford University Press, 1980).

Frampton, Kenneth, "Towards a Critical Regionalism: Six Points for an Architecture of Resistance." In *The Anti-Aesthetic: Essays on Postmodern Culture*, ed. Hal Foster (Bay Press: Seattle, 1983).

Fromm, Erich, *Escape From Freedom* (New York: Avon Books, 1941).

Gandelsonas, Diana and Agrest, Mario, "Semiotics and Architecture: Idelogical Consumption or Theoretical Work," *Opposition*, 1 (1973), 94.

Giedion, S., *Space, Time and Architecture* (Cambridge, MA: Harvard University Press, 1962).

Giedion, S., *The Eternal Present: The Beginnings of Architecture* (New York: Bollinger Series, 1964).

Giurgola, Romaldo, *Boston City Hall Competition Report.* Competition brief (Boston: Mitchell/Giurgola Asso. Architects, 1962).

Giurgola, Romaldo, "Notes on Architecture and Morality," *Precis, Journal of Columbia University Graduate School of Architecture and Planning*, 2 (1980), 51–52.

Giurgola, Romaldo and Mehta, Jaimini, *Louis I. Kahn, Architect* (Boulder: Westview Press, 1975).

Habermas, Jurgen, "Modernity: An Incomplete Project." In *The Anti-Aesthetic: Essays on Postmodern Culture*, ed. Hal Foster (Seattle: Bay Press, 1983), 3–15.

Heisenberg, Werner, *Physics and Beyond* (New York: Harper & Row, 1971).

Hirianna, M., *Outline of Indian Philosophy* (New Delhi: Motilal Banarasidas, 1993).

Horton, Heather, "Alberti, Sant'Andrea in Mantua," *Khan Academy*, available at: https://www.khanacademy.org/humanities/renaissance-reformation/early-renaissance1/sculpture-architecture-florence/a/alberti-santandrea-in-mantua.

Huxtable, Ada Louise, "The Architects Design Their 'Dream' Home," *New York Times Sunday Edition* (July 12, 1970).

Jameson, F., "The Constraints of Postmodernism." In *Rethinking Architecture: A Reader in Cultural Theory*, ed. N. Leach (London: Routledge, 1997).

Kelvin, Lord William, *Lord Kelvin Quotations*, available at: http://http://zapatopi.net/kelvin/quotes/.

Kramrisch, Stella, *A Survey of Painting in the Deccan* (New Delhi: Munshiram Manoharlal Publishers, 1983).

Lefaivre, Liane and Tzonis, Alexander, *Critical Regionalism, Architecture and Identity in a Globalized World* (Munich, Berlin, London and New York: Prestel, 2003).

Lévi-Strauss, Claude, *Structural Anthropology* (New York: Anchor Books, 1967).

Lévi-Strauss, Claude, *The Savage Mind, Nature of Human Society* (Chicago: University of Chicago Press, 1966).

McEvilley, Thomas, *The Shape of Ancient Thought* (New York: Allworth Press, 2002).

Marcuse, Herbert, "Art as a Form of Reality." In *On the Future of Art*, ed. Edward F. Fry (New York: The Viking Press, 1970), 123–134.

Marcuse, Herbert, *One-Dimensional Man, Studies in Ideology of Advanced Industrial Society* (Boston: Beacon Press, 1968).

Martin, Ronald E., *American Literature and the Destruction of Knowledge* (Durham, NC: Duke University Press, 1991).

Mehta, Jaimini, *Rethinking Modernity, Towards Post-Rational Architecture* (New Delhi: Niyogi Books, 2011).

Mohanty, Jitendra Nath, "The Concept of Rationality." In *Phenomenology and Indian Philosophy*, ed. Lester Embree, J. Mohanty and D.P. Chattopadhyaya (Albany: State University of New York Press, 1992), 10–17.

Mohanty, Jitendra Nath, *The Empirical and the Transcendental*, ed. Bina Gupta (Lanham: Rowman & Littlefield, 2000).

Naruda, Pablo, *Towards the Splendid City: Nobel Lecture* (New York: Farrar, Straus & Giroux, 1972).

National Gallery of Victoria, *Vienna Art and Design* (Melbourne: National Gallery of Victoria, 2011).

Norberg-Schulz, Christian, *Genius Loci* (New York: Rizzoli, 1980).

Pallasmaa, Juhani, *The Eyes of the Skin* (London: John Wiley & Sons, 2005).

Pant, Vrinda, "Architecture and Dance," (undergraduate dissertation, School of Architecture, CEPT University, 1999).

Pinker, Steven, "Science Is Not Your Enemy," *New Republic* (Aug. 7, 2013), available at: https://newrepublic.com/article/114127/science-not-enemy-humanities.

Popper, Karl R., "Of Clouds and Clocks." In *Objective Knowledge: An Evolutionary Approach* (London: Oxford University Press, 1972), 206–255.

Py-Lieberman, Beth, "The Really Big Art of Claes Oldenburg," *Smithsonian Magazine* (Aug. 1995), available at: www.smithsonianmag.com/arts-culture.html.

Ricoeur, Paul, *History and Truth* (Evanston: Northwestern University Press, 1965).

Rocher, Ludo, *The Puranas* (Wiesbaden: Otto Harrassowitz, 1986).

Rykwert, Joseph and Tavernor, R., "Sant'Andrea, Mantua," *The Architect's Journal* (21 May 1986), 36–57.

Saussure, Ferdinand de, *Course in General Linguistics*, ed. Charles Bally and Albert Sechehaye (New York: McGraw-Hill Book Company, 1966).

Scholem, Gershom, *Major Trends in Jewish Mysticism* (New York: Schocken Books, 1974).

Schumacher, John, *Human Posture: The Nature of Inquiry* (New York: SUNY Press, 1989).

Sennett, Richard, *The Uses of Disorder, Personal Identity and City Life* (New York: Vintage Books, 1970).

Stein, Gertrude, *Picasso* (London: B.T. Batsford, 1939).

Stephens, Suzanne, "A.I.A. HQ: Magnificent Intentions," *Architectural Forum*, 140(3) (Oct. 1973), 36–43.

Timms, Edward, "The Golden Ages of Jewish Austro-Hungary," *Times Literary Supplement* (Feb. 20, 2013).

Tyrwhitt, Jacqueline, "The Moving Eye." In *Explorations in Communication*, ed. Edmund Carpenter and Marshall McLuhan (Boston: Beacon Press, 1960), 90–95.

Urbahn, Max O., "Evolution of the Octagon Building," *AIA Journal* (June 1973), 46–53.

Vitruvius, *The Ten Books on Architecture*, trans. Morris Morgan (New York: Dover Publications, 1960).

Washington Post, "Architects' Own Office Plan Rejected," *Washington Post* (Sept. 24, 1968).

Wikipedia, "Boston City Hall," available at: https://en.wikipedia.org/wiki/Boston_City_Hall.

Illustration Credits

Introduction
Figure 0.1   Studio Jaimini Mehta
Figure 0.2   Studio Jaimini Mehta

Chapter 1
Figure 1.1   Jaimini Mehta
Figure 1.2   https://commons.wikimedia.org/w/index.php?curid=335443
Figure 1.3   © F.L.C. / Adagp, Paris, 2016. Photo: ADAGP Image Bank
Figure 1.4   Jaimini Mehta
Figure 1.5   Homann, Johann Baptist, 1663–1724
Figure 1.6   Jordy Meow
Figure 1.7   Charles Dominique Joseph Eisen
Figure 1.8   Jaimini Mehta
Figure 1.9   Courtesy of Claes Oldenberg
Figure 1.10   Jaimini Mehta
Figure 1.11   Michigan Department of Transportation

Chapter 2
Figure 2.1   Charles-François Daubigny
Figure 2.2   Anonymous (Artist unknown)

Chapter 5
Figure 5.1   https://commons.wikimedia.org/w/index.php?curid=29793041

Chapter 6
Figure 6.1   Karl Richard Lepsius
Figure 6.2   Fra Paolino the Minorite
Figure 6.3   Georges Perrot and Charles Chipiez
Figure 6.4   Punita Mehta
Figure 6.5   Punita Mehta

Chapter 7

Figure 7.1	Jaimini Mehta
Figure 7.2	Jaimini Mehta
Figure 7.3	Jaimini Mehta
Figure 7.4	Courtesy of Vrinda Makwana Pant
Figure 7.5	Courtesy of Vrinda Makwana Pant
Figure 7.6	Jaimini Mehta
Figure 7.7	Jaimini Mehta
Figure 7.8	Jaimini Mehta
Figure 7.9	Jaimini Mehta

Chapter 9

Figure 9.1	© F.L.C. / Adagp, Paris, 1920 sauf pour l"égllsed de Flrminy: © F.L.C. / Adagp, Paris, et Jose Oubrerie
Figure 9.2	Jaimini Mehta
Figure 9.3	Jaimini Mehta
Figure 9.4	© F.L.C. / Adagp, Paris, 1925 sauf pour l"égllsed de Flrminy: © F.L.C. / Adagp, Paris, et Jose Oubrerie
Figure 9.5	© F.L.C. / Adagp, Paris, 1925 sauf pour l"égllsed de Flrminy: © F.L.C. / Adagp, Paris, et Jose Oubrerie
Figure 9.6	© F.L.C. / Adagp, Paris, 1960 sauf pour l"égllsed de Flrminy: © F.L.C. / Adagp, Paris, et Jose Oubrerie
Figure 9.7	Jaimini Mehta
Figure 9.8	© F.L.C. / Adagp, Paris, 1955 sauf pour l"égllsed de Flrminy: © F.L.C. / Adagp, Paris, et Jose Oubrerie
Figure 9.9	Creative Commons. Share Alike 3.0 Unported
Figure 9.10	© F.L.C. / Adagp, Paris, 1927 sauf pour l"égllsed de Flrminy: © F.L.C. / Adagp, Paris, et Jose Oubrerie
Figure 9.11	Jaimini Mehta
Figure 9.12	Jaimini Mehta
Figure 9.13	Jaimini Mehta
Figure 9.14	Jaimini Mehta
Figure 9.15	Jaimini Mehta
Figure 9.16	Jaimini Mehta

Chapter 10

Figure 10.1	Louis I. Kahn Collection, University of Pennsylvania and the Pennsylvania Historical and Museum Commission
Figure 10.2	Louis I. Kahn Collection, University of Pennsylvania and the Pennsylvania Historical and Museum Commission
Figure 10.3	Courtesy of Vastu Shilpa Foundation
Figure 10.4	Courtesy of Vastu Shilpa Foundation
Figure 10.5	Courtesy of Vastu Shilpa Foundation
Figure 10.6	Courtesy of Vastu Shilpa Foundation
Figure 10.7	Courtesy of Vastu Shilpa Foundation
Figure 10.8	Courtesy of Vastu Shilpa Foundation
Figure 10.9	Courtesy of Vastu Shilpa Foundation

Figure 10.10   Courtesy of Vastu Shilpa Foundation
Figure 10.11   Courtesy of Vastu Shilpa Foundation

Chapter 11

Figure 11.1   Courtesy of The Architectural Archives, University of Pennsylvania
Figure 11.2   Jaimini Mehta
Figure 11.3   Jaimini Mehta
Figure 11.4   Jaimini Mehta
Figure 11.5   Louis I. Kahn Collection, University of Pennsylvania and the Pennsylvania Historical and Museum Commission
Figure 11.6   Jaimini Mehta
Figure 11.7   Mitchell/Giurgola Collection, The Architectural Archives, University of Pennsylvania
Figure 11.8   Public Domain
Figure 11.9   Jaimini Mehta
Figure 11.10   Mitchell/Giurgola Collection, The Architectural Archives, University of Pennsylvania
Figure 11.11   Mitchell/Giurgola Collection, The Architectural Archives, University of Pennsylvania
Figure 11.12   Mitchell/Giurgola Collection, The Architectural Archives, University of Pennsylvania
Figure 11.13   Mitchell/Giurgola Collection, The Architectural Archives, University of Pennsylvania
Figure 11.14   Jaimini Mehta
Figure 11.15   Mitchell/Giurgola Collection, The Architectural Archives, University of Pennsylvania
Figure 11.16   Jaimini Mehta
Figure 11.17   Mitchell/Giurgola Collection, The Architectural Archives, University of Pennsylvania
Figure 11.18   Mitchell/Giurgola Collection, The Architectural Archives, University of Pennsylvania
Figure 11.19   Mitchell/Giurgola Collection, The Architectural Archives, University of Pennsylvania
Figure 11.20   Mitchell/Giurgola Collection, The Architectural Archives, University of Pennsylvania
Figure 11.21   Jaimini Mehta
Figure 11.22   Mitchell/Giurgola Collection, The Architectural Archives, University of Pennsylvania
Figure 11.23   Mitchell/Giurgola Collection, The Architectural Archives, University of Pennsylvania
Figure 11.24   Mitchell/Giurgola Collection, The Architectural Archives, University of Pennsylvania
Figure 11.25   Mitchell/Giurgola Collection, The Architectural Archives, University of Pennsylvania
Figure 11.26   Mitchell/Giurgola Collection, The Architectural Archives, University of Pennsylvania
Figure 11.27   Mitchell/Giurgola Collection, The Architectural Archives, University of Pennsylvania

Index

Note: page numbers in italics denote figures.